ASSESSING
ASSESSMENT

*INTUITION OR
EVIDENCE?*

ASSESSING ASSESSMENT

Series Editor:
Harry Torrance, University of Sussex

The aim of this series is to take a longer term view of current developments in assessment and to interrogate them in terms of research evidence deriving from both theoretical and empirical work. The intention is to provide a basis for testing the rhetoric of current policy and for the development of well-founded practice.

Current titles

ASSESSING
ASSESSMENT

INTUITION OR EVIDENCE?

TEACHERS AND NATIONAL ASSESSMENT OF SEVEN-YEAR-OLDS

Caroline Gipps,
Margaret Brown,
Bet McCallum and
Shelley McAlister

Open University Press
Buckingham · Philadelphia

Open University Press
Celtic Court
22 Ballmoor
Buckingham
MK18 1XW

and
1900 Frost Road, Suite 101
Bristol, PA 19007, USA

First Published 1995

A catalogue record of this book is available from the British Library

ISBN 0 335 19383 8 (pb)   0 335 19384 6 (hb)

Library of Congress Cataloging-in-Publication Data
Intuition or evidence? : teachers and national assessment of seven year
   olds / by Caroline Gipps . . . [et al.].
      p. cm. — (Assessing assessment)
   Includes bibliographical references and index.
   ISBN 0–335–19384–6. — ISBN 0–335–19383–8 (pbk.)
      1. Educational tests and measurements — Great Britain.
   2. Students — Great Britain — Rating of. 3. Education, Elementary —
   Great Britain — Evaluation. I. Gipps, C.V. II. Series.
   LB3056.G7I58   1995
   372.12′64′0941 — dc20   95–10788
                                                                    CIP

Typeset by Colset Pte Ltd, Singapore
Printed in Great Britain by St Edmundsbury Press Ltd,
Bury St Edmunds, Suffolk.

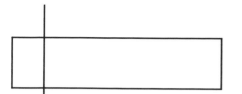

CONTENTS

SERIES EDITOR'S INTRODUCTION

Changing theories and methods of assessment have been the focus of significant attention for some years now, not only in the United Kingdom, but also in many other western industrial countries and many developing countries. Curriculum developers have realized that real change will not take place in schools if traditional paper-and-pencil tests, be they essay or multiple choice, remain unchanged to exert a constraining influence on how teachers and pupils approach new curricula. Similarly, examiners have been concerned to develop more valid and 'authentic' ways of assessing the changes which have been introduced into school syllabuses over recent years – more practical work, oral work, problem solving and so forth. In turn, psychologists and sociologists have become concerned with the impact of assessment on learning and motivation, and how that impact can be developed more positively. This has led to a myriad of developments in the field of assessment, often involving an increasing role for the teacher in school-based assessment, as more relevant and challenging tasks are devised by examination agencies for administration by teachers in schools, and as the role and status of more routine teacher assessment of coursework, practical work, groupwork and so forth has become enhanced.

However, educationists have not been the only ones to focus much more closely on the interrelation of curriculum, pedagogy and assessment. Governments around the world, but particularly in the UK, have also begun to take a close interest in the ways in which assessment can influence and even control teaching, and in the changes in curriculum and teaching which could be brought about by changes in assessment. This interest has not been wholly coherent. Government intervention in the UK has sometimes initiated, sometimes reinforced the move towards a more practical and vocationally-oriented curriculum and thus the move towards more practical, school-based assessment. But government has also been concerned with issues of accountability and with what it sees as the maintenance of traditional academic standards through the use of externally set tests. The overall effect has been that as certain sorts of responsibility for assessment have been devolved to school level, the parameters within which such responsibility can be exercised have been more tightly drawn. As the Dearing Report (1993) on the National Curriculum put it: 'Teachers want to be trusted ... but the corollary of trust is accountability ... we need a reliable means by which [we] ... can evaluate the effectiveness of individual schools and the education system as a whole'.

It is precisely because of the contradictions and complexity inherent in current developments that the present series of books on assessment has been developed. Many claims are being made with respect to the efficacy of new approaches to assessment which require careful review and investigation. Likewise many changes are being required by government intervention which may lead to hurried and poorly understood developments being implemented in schools, not the least of which are revisions to the National Curriculum and its testing arrangements recommended by Dearing. The aim of this series is to take a longer term view of the changes which are occurring, to move beyond the immediate problems of implementation and to interrogate the claims and the changes in terms of broader research evidence which derives from both theoretical and empirical work. In reviewing the field in this way the intention of the series is thus to highlight relevant research evidence, identify key factors and principles which should underpin the developments taking place, and provide teachers and administrators with a basis for informed decision-making which takes the educational issues seriously and goes beyond simply accommodating the latest policy imperative.

This new book by Caroline Gipps, Margaret Brown and their colleagues at The London Institute of Education and King's College, is particularly relevant to this task. The book reports on a research project, funded by the Economic and Social Research Council (ESRC), which was explicitly designed to investigate the impact on primary schools of the National Curriculum assessment arrangements embodied in the 1988 Education Act. The book focuses on the assessment arrangements at Key Stage 1 in particular, reporting on both the conduct and impact of Standard Assessment Tasks, and on the development of Teacher Assessment. However, the research also offers many insights beyond the specific impact of certain testing procedures on certain classrooms. The book explores the impact of testing on the curriculum and teaching more generally, and investigates to what extent assessment arrangements can and should be standardized for very young children. It also identifies and analyses teachers' developing beliefs, understandings, and actual practices with respect to the assessment of young children, and generates a powerful critique of overly mechanistic approaches to the use of assessment in school reform.

Not that the book is wholly critical of government policy. Significant attention is given to the issues of raising standards of achievement and there is some sympathy for the Task Group on Assessment and Testing (TGAT) Report's original recommendations. Observations and interview data which indicate the development of systematic approaches to teacher assessment involving careful planning and the gathering of evidence, are also presented, as are findings which suggest that some of the original, broader Standard Assessment Tasks had a positive impact on teachers' perceptions of the possibilities of assessment. However, it is also clear from the data that teachers were operating from very different beliefs about what is appropriate to young children than was TGAT, and that the potentially positive impact of flexible and practical approaches to testing is likely to be all too easily and quickly reversed by the introduction of narrower paper-and-pencil tests of 'the basics'.

The strength of the book lies in its detailed investigation of teachers' beliefs about assessment and how those beliefs interact with and mediate government policy, often with unintended and unanticipated consequences. Analysts and commentators on assessment have been increasingly ready to assume rather than investigate the impact of assessment procedures on teaching and learning, and to argue that it should be a policy priority to design assessment systems in such a way that the impact is positive, underpinning rather than undermining good teaching. Caroline Gipps and colleagues demonstrate that this is easier said than done. The book provides a wealth of evidence about the consequences of intervening in this way and suggests that such improvements as can be identified derive as much from the process of teachers working together in order to understand the intervention, as from the intervention itself.

Harry Torrance

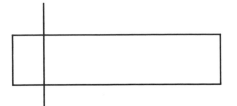

ACKNOWLEDGEMENTS

The research reported here was funded by a grant from the Economic and Social Research Council (R000 23 2192). We are most grateful to the ESRC for its support and for funding the second phase of the study.

We are indebted to the schools and LEAs with whom we worked over the period 1990–94 for their co-operation and support. Although we tried to restrict our demands on teachers' and heads' time, they were nevertheless considerable.

We should like to thank Susan Stocker for her stalwart work in typing and reprocessing this manuscript.

Finally, our thanks go to Harry Torrance, the series editor, for his patient support and painstaking editing.

ABBREVIATIONS

APU	Assessment of Performance Unit
AT	attainment target
CATS	Consortium for Assessment and Testing in Schools
DES	Department of Education and Science
DfE	Department for Education
ESRC	Economic and Social Research Council
GCSE	General Certificate of Secondary Education
HMI	Her Majesty's Inspectorate
ILEA	Inner London Education Authority
INSET	in-service education for teachers
LEA	local education authority
NAHT	National Association of Head Teachers
NAPS	National Assessment in Primary Schools: An Evaluation
NAS/UWT	National Association of Schoolmasters/Union of Women Teachers
NFER	National Foundation for Educational Research
NUT	National Union of Teachers
OFSTED	Office for Standards in Education
PLR	Primary Language Record

RoA	record of achievement
SAT	standard assessment task
SCAA	Schools Curriculum and Assessment Authority
SEAC	Schools Examinations and Assessment Council
SoA	statement of attainment
TA	teacher assessment
TGAT	Task Group on Assessment and Testing

SETTING THE
SCENE

This book is about what happened in schools when a compulsory national assessment programme was introduced in England for children of six and seven years of age – that is, in the second year of formal schooling. In the research study (National Assessment in Primary School: an evaluation (NAPS) funded by a grant from the ESRC, reference no. R000 23 2192) which informs these chapters, we focused on teachers' assessment practice and how this changed and developed as a result of the national assessment programme. The implications of our findings, however, go wider than the seemingly narrow remit of infant teachers' assessment practice – our research and analysis offer insights into:

- the impact of testing on the curriculum;
- how schools with small numbers of staff work together to deal with change;
- teachers' views of learning/teaching and assessing; and
- the role of criterion referencing and of teacher assessment (TA) within it.

This information also forms the basis for a developing model of educational assessment. The backdrop to the study was the introduction of national assessment and the effect of this major innovation on teachers, but the study looked more broadly at teachers' assessment skills, understanding and beliefs, as well as their actual practice. Research on assessment in primary schools in the early 1980s (Gipps *et al.* 1983) had shown that teachers' understanding of issues in assessment was very limited; while there was widespread use of standardized tests of reading and maths, there was little understanding of how the scores were derived, or what they meant, and no understanding of issues such as reliability and validity. Their own assessments were intuitive and discursive, rather than against criteria, and often not written down; teachers found it hard to articulate their assessment practice.

The study which this book describes sets out to see what happened to primary teachers' assessment practice when they were faced with the demands of national assessment; with little training and few materials, how did these teachers carry out the hundreds of teacher assessments required of them? How did they manage the standard assessment tasks (SATs), and what did 'standard' mean in this setting? Given the legal requirement to assess, coupled with the very high profile that came with reporting to parents and the publication of league tables, how did teachers react? Did they become 'technicians' administering external tests (as they were in the early 1980s) or did they engage with the issues and become skilled assessors? We wanted to find out how teachers and schools coped with the imposed change and how the results were used. We also wanted to know whether teachers thought the assessments suggested were appropriate for young children and whether the age of the children influenced their ways of doing the assessments.

The first run of assessment for seven-year-olds in English, maths and science took place in 1991, with the second run in 1992. By the time 1993 came along the scope of the assessment programme and the time it took had been dramatically reduced, but many schools, as a result of a national boycott organized by the three largest teacher unions, either did not carry out the testing or did not report the results to their local education authorities (LEAs). Our study, therefore, focused on assessment practice in 1991 and 1992 and, to a lesser extent, in 1993 (because of the boycott). In 1994 the boycott continued, but we asked our teachers and heads for a retrospective of the previous four years.

The wider backdrop to this book includes two different developing educational themes: first, our understandings about educational (as opposed to psychometric) assessment; and second, the impact of government policy on education standards and teachers' and schools' behaviour. This study of the national assessment programme teaches us much about the large-scale assessment of young children, how teachers actually make their own informal assessments, and philosophies of assessment, teaching and learning among teachers at Key Stage 1 (ages 5–7). These lessons have implications for all who are involved in developing policy or practice in primary schools and in the wider field of assessment.

The 'Intuition or Evidence?' of the title is a theme which runs through the book; teachers' assessments at the start were largely intuitive, and while some teachers now still make intuitive judgements, others base them firmly on evidence. The changes in government policy, on the other hand, and the demands for testing and publication of results to raise standards seem to be based on intuition rather than any evidence. Indeed, by the end of the study our evidence shows that a number of headteachers thought that standards of teaching and learning had improved, but as a result of many different factors and not in the simplistic way envisaged.

We now set the scene by describing further the national assessment programme and its introduction.

Raising standards and expectations

In this section we look at why the government introduced a national assessment programme so that we can, in later chapters, evaluate the extent to which its aims have been achieved. Concern about standards in education in recent times began to be voiced in 1976 with the speech given at Ruskin College by the then Labour Prime Minister, James Callaghan. In it he argued that curriculum, standards and accountability of schools were issues of national importance which should be open to debate. The Green Paper *Education in Schools: A Consultative Document* (DES 1977) which followed it had a major section entitled 'Standards and Assessment'. In this, the case for 'a coherent and soundly based means of assessment for the education system, for schools, and for individual pupils' (p. 16) was argued. However, the efforts of the new Conservative government in the following decade focused on reforming the examination system at 16+ to give a unified GCSE, relying on the work of the Assessment of Performance Unit (APU), HMI and public examinations to give a picture of national standards (Daugherty 1994). The 1977 Green Paper, issued by a Labour government, had rejected the regular testing of all pupils in basic skills, national monitoring of standards, and performance tables enabling parents and the public to compare schools. Within ten years these were explicitly to be part of the policy of the Conservative government. The detailed political and policy argument which took place during those ten years is well described by both Daugherty (1994) and Ball (1990).

The 1985 White Paper *Better Schools* (DES 1985), issued by Sir Keith Joseph, concentrated on raising standards and contained the first suggestion that national attainment targets, accompanied by some form of national assessment, should be introduced into the final years of primary school, to parallel the national criteria which had been introduced for the new GCSE. These criteria were the first direct intervention by a government in the control of the content of curriculum and examinations in the twentieth century; previously examination syllabuses had been determined by the independent examination boards.

Following on from *Better Schools*, a one-year feasibility study (1986–7) was set up to investigate *Attainment Targets and Assessment in the Primary Phase* (Denvir et al. 1987). Mathematics was taken as the subject of this, following some outcry over the publication of HMI objectives for the teaching of English. However, in autumn 1986 a new education minister, Kenneth Baker, was appointed; without waiting for the results of the feasibility study, he announced the decision to impose a national curriculum in January 1987 and outlined plans for the national curriculum and accompanying national assessment in April that year. These resulted in the publication of *The National Curriculum 5–16: A Consultation Document* (DES 1987), which described in general terms a national curriculum backed by clear assessment standards which would form part of an Education Bill to be introduced later the same year. In this document the following claim about assessment and raising standards was made:

> 7 ... Pupils should be entitled to the same opportunities wherever they go to school, and standards of attainment must be raised throughout England and Wales.

8 A national curriculum backed by clear assessment arrangements will help to raise standards of attainment by
  (i) ensuring that all pupils study a broad and balanced range of subjects . . .
  (ii) setting clear objectives for what children over the full range of ability should be able to achieve . . .
  (iv) checking on progress towards those objectives and performance achieved at various stages, so that pupils can be stretched further when they are doing well and given more help when they are not. . . .

23 Attainment targets will be set for all three core subjects of mathematics, English and science. These will establish what children should normally be expected to know, understand and be able to do at around the ages of 7, 11, 14 and 16, and will enable the progress of each child to be measured against established national standards. They will reflect what pupils must achieve to progress in their education and to become thinking and informed people. The range of attainment targets should cater for all the full ability range and be sufficiently challenging *at all levels* to raise expectations, particularly of pupils of middling achievement who frequently are not challenged enough, as well as stretching and stimulating the most able. This is a proven and essential way towards raising standards of achievement. Targets must be sufficiently specific for pupils, teachers, parents and others to have a clear idea of what is expected, and to provide a sound basis for assessment.

(DES 1987: 3–4, 9–10)

The consultation document led directly to the sections on national curriculum and assessment in the Education Reform Act of 1988.

The Education Reform Act was a significant plank of government reform policy, and a key aspect of this reform was a national curriculum and assessment programme. Through the Act the government wished to restructure the education system, to introduce parental choice and market forces into the education system and, ultimately, to improve the quality of education and to raise standards in order to overcome Britain's economic problems. Concern about the range of curriculum experiences offered to pupils in different schools and low expectations of pupils' performance had been regularly voiced by the HMI. The widespread demise of the 11+ selection test following the introduction of comprehensive schools in the 1960s and 1970s meant that there were now no formal assessments required in the education system before the public examinations at 16. The lack of an examination or national system of testing at the end of primary school left this sector of schooling wide open to criticism of performance standards across the primary age range (5–11). The national curriculum was introduced to make sure that pupils of compulsory school age followed the same programmes of study, with English, mathematics and science forming the core, and other subjects – history, geography, technology, art, music and PE (and, at secondary level, a modern foreign language) – making up the ten foundation subjects. Religious education remained compulsory, but with a different framework for determining syllabuses. National assessment was always seen as a crucial aspect of the national curriculum programme, for without it the national curriculum could not be easily enforced. Through the publication of the results of national assessment at the key ages of 7, 11 and 14, together with GCSE taken at age 16, it was anticipated by the government that teachers would be both forced to cover the national curriculum and concentrate on teaching and raising standards of basic skills.

A leaflet for parents in 1991 made this point:

> These tests are all part of the new national curriculum which lays down what your child should learn in the most important subjects as he or she progresses through school. The national curriculum aims to raise the standards of *all* pupils. The new tests are the key.

> (DES 1990)

However, by 1992 the next version of this leaflet softened the claims:

> We all want our children to achieve higher standards. The National Curriculum is designed to achieve this by setting demanding national targets for pupils of all ages and abilities. National tests, being introduced at the ages of 7, 11 and 14, will check how your child is progressing against the National Curriculum targets.

> (DES 1992)

By 1993 HMI articulated the same belief but gave a little more detail on how this would operate. In this quotation, the continued division between HMI (now OFSTED), which emphasized the importance of the formative ongoing functions of TA, and the DES, which favoured the summative, end-of-key-stage testing as the major influence, is illustrated:

Assessment and standards of work
The assessment requirements of the national curriculum have a vital role in raising the expectations of teachers, pupils and parents. In particular, assessment should ensure that individual learning is more clearly targeted and that shortcomings are quickly identified and remedied, thus contributing towards higher standards overall.
(Office of Her Majesty's Chief Inspector/OFSTED 1993)

As Murphy (1990) and other observers put it, national assessment was to have a key role in the move to raise education standards by giving greater choice to the consumers (parents) and encouraging them to use this by supplying them with clearer, and more regular, information about pupils' attainments. Brehony (1990) argues that the New Right, faced by the (to them) mysterious and unknown world of primary schooling, reverted to common sense or popular nostrums about the efficacy of paper and pencil tests and discipline. But in earlier work (Gipps 1988a) it was argued that the proposal by the Task Group in Assessment and Testing (TGAT), though educative in scope and recognizing the particular nature of primary schooling and the needs of young children, was forced to harness its approach to assessment to the highly competitive arrangements required by the Education Reform Act.

As well as bringing in an assessment system to monitor pupil performance and help the teaching process, a key development was the use of assessment to evaluate teachers and schools. This can be traced through to one of the requirements for the TGAT group, which was to provide what the DES termed 'informative assessment', meaning that assessment evidence should be available which could inform the system on the performance of schools and teachers.

A significant factor in the call for an improvement in education standards was a report published in 1983 comparing performance in mathematics standards in schools in England and West Germany. The authors compared English data from an international survey of performance in 1964 and data from German final examinations, using this to claim that German pupils in the bottom half of the ability range obtained levels of performance comparable with the average for the whole ability range in England (Prais and Wagner 1983). A number of other international comparisons also showed that English schools were no higher than mid-way in the league tables. The APU, which had carried out anonymous testing of 'light' samples of pupils, had been unable to comment satisfactorily on whether national standards were appropriate, or even whether they were rising or falling (Gipps and Goldstein 1983). These international studies brought into play the issue of comparison of English schools with those of other countries, a politically very powerful argument within the context of discussions about economic decline.

It is important to look at the link between testing and raising standards in education, the implicit belief being that introducing an assessment programme will ipso facto raise standards. The publication of exam results has, since 1980, been seen as one way of *maintaining* standards. We know that the imposition of assessments or exams which are very important for either pupils or teachers will have a direct effect on what and how teachers teach (Gipps 1994) but, as we will go on to investigate in more detail later, it is important not to have too simplistic a model of how this operates.

In 1980 the Education Act required secondary schools to publish 16+ examination results, a major element of the Conservatives' manifesto being that parents using the state sector of education should have more information and choice in deciding which schools their children should attend. Thus from 1982 the annual publication of public examination results at 16 and 18 was made compulsory. This built on a fairly widespread belief that schools should be more accountable to the communities they serve and that the publication of examination results would help to bring this about. However, the different ways schools chose of presenting their results still made comparisons very difficult for parents or the local press. Subsequently, in 1992, schools were required to report results publicly in an identical format so that league tables of schools' performance could easily be produced. In addition, the DfE produced annual sets of national league tables for schools based on pupils' combined grades across subjects at GCSE and Advanced levels. The problems with using 'raw' examination results to evaluate school performance have been described in detail elsewhere (Goldstein and Cuttance

1988; Gipps and Stobart 1993). Notwithstanding the debate about the importance of looking at school intake and at progress ('value added') by the school as the basis for school performance league tables, in 1991 and 1992 league tables were published of LEAs' performance in the national assessment programme of seven-year-olds. The TGAT report (DES 1988) had specifically advised against reporting results at Key Stage 1 and the Education Reform Act itself did not specifically require reporting of results at this age. By 1991 there was an intention to publish league tables for seven-year-olds. However, by late 1993 the DfE withdrew from this, although not from publication of age 11 results, under pressure from the boycott called by the teacher unions. What is clear is that some infant teachers were distressed at the thought of the results of such young children being made publicly available, even at classroom and school level.

Thus we can trace a clear line of argument in favour of national assessment as a way of raising standards and expectations. Of course, few people – parents, teachers or other voters – would not be in favour of such an end. There is less consensus, however, as to the best means to achieve it and the extent to which imposed, legislated testing will genuinely raise education standards, or whether it will simply raise test scores at the expense of better education.

Assessment in primary schools

In a wide-scale study of teachers' use of standardized tests carried out in 1980 and 1981, it became clear that there was a considerable amount of testing going on. At least 79% of all LEAs required their primary schools to test children, at ages 7, 8 and/or 11, in reading and/or maths. In addition to this, many primary schools chose to use other tests at other ages (Gipps *et al.* 1983). Having carried out this level of testing, schools did little with the results beyond putting them into record books and using them to identify children for remedial help; little or no use was made of them for modifying teaching or curriculum – what we now call formative assessment. Similarly, Close and Brown (1987) found at secondary level that teachers considered themselves to be better informed about their pupils' learning as a result of diagnostic assessment, but were often unwilling to adapt the curriculum in response.

The survey of testing practice (Gipps *et al.* 1983) also found a lack of knowledge and understanding generally about testing practice and the uses of assessment. British primary school teachers were, at that time, unsophisticated in their approach to assessment. The picture that emerges of primary school practice at that time was of testing (with reading tests, standardized maths tests, etc. and teachers' own tests), record-keeping and marking of work making up the teachers' repertoire for evaluating pupils' performance. However, the results of the concern about standards during the late 1970s, and some filtering down of ideas about profiling and records of achievement from secondary schools, had led to a sprinkling of LEA initiatives in the area of assessment. In the feasibility study for national assessment in primary schools (Denvir, Brown & Eve 1987), reference is made to the earlier production and large-scale implementation within the Inner London Education Authority (ILEA) of a 'Checkpoints' scheme which involved one-to-one and small-group assessment of specific mathematical concepts and skills. They also describe more recent schemes under development in four other LEAs, including a variety of modes of testing for written tests (both graded and traditional), practical group tests and ongoing profiling. At the same time the ILEA was developing and testing a Primary Language Record (PLR), on a profiling model. Nevertheless, assessment, we would argue, involving teachers' *informal* assessment of pupils' attainment and understanding, based on observation and questioning, is largely a post-1988 concept at primary level. Thomas (1990: 111) describes it thus:

> Overwhelmingly, assessment is relatively detailed, informal and undertaken in the course of the day's work. Assessment of this kind is probably one of the most difficult parts of a teacher's job, but far less time is given to it in initial training and in in-service training than is given to discussing child development in general terms ... I ... call this aspect of assessment *informal assessment*.

The TGAT report was also clearly envisaging a much broader role for assessment than testing, as this definition of 'assessment' indicates:

> A general term enhancing all methods customarily used to appraise performance of an individual pupil or a group. It

may refer to a broad appraisal including many sources of evidence and many aspects of a pupil's knowledge, understanding, skills and attitudes; or to a particular occasion or instrument. An assessment instrument may be any method or procedure, formal or informal, for producing information about pupils: e.g. a written test paper, an interview schedule, a measurement task using equipment, a class quiz.

(DES 1988: Preface and Glossary)

Harlen (1983: vii) argued for the importance of observation:

Assessment in education has been criticised for interfering with the process of learning, the analogy being that of a gardener constantly pulling up his plants to see if the roots are growing. There is some truth in this, particularly if there is too much assessment of the wrong kind, but it also distorts reality to make a point. Gardeners do have to find out if their plants are growing and they do this, not by uprooting them, but by careful observation with a knowledgeable eye, so that they can give water and food at the right time and avoid either undernourishment or over-watering.

By 1991, Conner was able to produce a 180-page book on methods or techniques for informal assessment of primary-aged children (Conner 1991). However, the general consensus seemed to be that much of the assessment made by primary teachers was intuitive. Given the absence of syllabus, bench-marks or criteria for teachers to focus on when evaluating pupils' performance, a lack of articulation, explication or systematic approach would not be surprising in the days before the national curriculum and assessment programme. The question which interested us was how practice changed, if it did, when the national assessment programme came in.

The introduction of national assessment

In 1988, parallel with the passing through Parliament of the Education Reform Act, the blueprint for the national assessment programme was published in the TGAT report (DES 1988). The national assessment programme, as outlined in the TGAT report, required pupils to be assessed against the national curriculum attainment targets both through external tests (originally called SATs), and by their teachers through TA, and the final results to be published at the ages of 7, 11 and 14; that is, at the end of Key Stages One (5–7), Two (7–11) and Three (11–14). The results from the two aspects of the assessment programme, teacher assessment and the SATs were to be combined using a system of moderation to draw the teachers' assessment into line with the test results where the two did not match.

An important aspect of the TGAT framework was that teachers' assessments would be central to the system; teachers were to assess pupils' performance continuously using their own informal methods and this assessment information would provide both formative and diagnostic information to support teaching. This TA would be summed up at the end of each key stage and used as part of the reporting programme. As Lawton (1992) points out, a major achievement of the TGAT report was to make a significant change in professional and public thinking in relation to ongoing assessment and the teacher's role in this.

Because of teachers' anxiety about testing young children and the fear of assessment at 11 bringing back a rigid 11+ testing system, the TGAT report was generally welcomed by teachers and educationists as it placed a firm emphasis on *formative teacher assessment*, assessment that was integrated with good curriculum and teaching practice. This formative assessment would help teachers in planning their work with individual pupils as well as classes, and would therefore incorporate a diagnostic process. (See Table 1 for some definitions of assessment terms.)

A second revolutionary element in the TGAT report was the *ten-level system*: the attainment targets (ATs) of the national curriculum were to be articulated at ten levels, covering the age range 7–16. The series of levels was designed to enable progression, and the understanding was that pupils would work their way through the levels, mostly at the pace of one level every two years, but with allowances for faster or slower progress for pupils of widely differing abilities. Thus, most pupils aged 7 would be at level 2 in the system, while most pupils of 11 would be at level 4, but some pupils at 7 could be working towards level 1 (having not yet reached it) while others could be already at level 4. The ATs were described at each of

Table 1   Glossary

Assessment	A wide range of methods for evaluating pupil performance and attainment, including formal testing and examination, practical and oral assessment and classroom-based assessment carried out by teachers.
Attainment target	One goal to be reached within a subject in the core curriculum, e.g. AT1 in English is Speaking and Listening.
Formative assessment	Takes place during the course of teaching and is used essentially to feed back into the teaching/learning process.
Statement of Attainment (SoA)	A SoA is one of the criteria required to reach and complete an Attainment Target.
Summative assessment	Takes place at the end of a term or a course and is used to provide information about how much students have learned and how well a course has worked.
Performance assessment	Assessment tasks which match the activities that pupils do in school, e.g. essay writing and practical tasks. Marking is not 'objective' but requires judgements to be made by assessors/examiners.
Reliability	The extent to which an assessment would produce the same, or similar, score on two occasions or if given by two assessors. This is the 'accuracy' with which an assessment measures the skill or attainment it is designed to measure.
Validity	The extent to which an assessment measures what it purports to measure. If an assessment does not measure what it is designed to measure then its use is misleading.
High-stakes testing	An examination or test that has significant consequences for pupils and/or teachers.

these ten levels by a series of assessment criteria, or statements of attainment (SoAs), and these were to form the basis of a broadly criterion-referenced assessment system.

The third innovatory feature of the national assessment programme was this emphasis on *criterion referencing* as opposed to the more usual norm referencing. Until the late 1980s much assessment reporting had been in relation to averages, or norms, so that pupil performance would be reported in relation to the performance of other pupils of the same age, giving, for example, above average or below average scores or reading ages. During the late 1970s and 1980s, however, moves began in England towards developing assessment systems which reported pupils' performance, not in relation to the performance of other pupils of similar age, but in relation to specified standards, grades or criteria. This followed earlier moves in the USA and in Scotland (Black and Dockrell, 1984; Brown 1980; Popham 1984).

A major problem with this form of assessment is to do with the level of specification of the criteria: if criteria are specified precisely so that they can be unambiguously assessed, the size of the assessment task becomes a problem. A very high number of assessment criteria can lead to overload and to fragmented teaching. On the other hand, assessment criteria which are too general and vague will cause problems in reliable and consistent assessment. The national assessment programme unfortunately fell into this trap, with far too many SoAs written into the curriculum and assessment programme; for example, at Key Stage 1 in 1991, covering levels 1, 2 and 3 in the three core subjects, there were a total of 228 assessment criteria. In theory, a teacher of seven-year-olds would have to have assessed many, if not all, of these 228 assessment criteria for a class of 30 children, when making TA judgements at the end of the second year of formal schooling. By 1994, because of the complexity of the assessment and the overloading of the timetable, the national curriculum and its assessment programme were subject to a formal review by Sir Ron Dearing; this review came about as a result of widespread anxiety about the programme, brought to a head by the teachers' boycott of the national assessment programme in summer 1993.

A further difficulty in national assessment was the problem of reporting a final assessment profile when both TA and external tests had been used to assess the same parts of the national curriculum.

The fourth innovation advocated in the TGAT report (DES 1988: paras 73–77) was a *scaling process* in which the results are used to adjust the distributions of teachers' assessments, a form of moderation. The proposal was that groups of teachers would meet and consider both the SAT results and TA results for groups of pupils. The task of the group would be to explore any mismatch between the two distributions; 'the general aim would be to adjust the overall teacher rating results to match the overall results of the national tests' (DES 1988: para. 74). Nevertheless, there was also provision to confirm the TA results if the group of teachers felt that the SAT results were flawed or unfair. This was an interesting model, combining group moderation processes and a statistical procedure. However, it was not the system that materialized since it was felt to be too complex and expensive (Brown 1991). In the end, where TA and SAT did not agree for a child it was decided that the test score alone would be used, thus showing that the government valued the scores on national tests more than those determined by ongoing TA.

The government requirement that 'objective' test assessment be used as the basis to determine the results of each individual pupil, rather than as a broad indicator as to whether the set of results for the whole school was at the right level, changed the role of and specification for the tests themselves. They could no longer broadly sample the SoAs at a particular level in a topic; they were now required to give more precise information about each child's performance. It was this change in role that led to the SATs having to become more comprehensive and thus longer and more detailed.

As a result of the review of the national curriculum and assessment by Sir Ron Dearing, the status of TA is, in theory, to be upgraded. The Dearing Review (Dearing 1993) recommended that equal standing be given to TA and test results and that both are reported to parents. Nevertheless, in published school league tables at age 11, and unpublished local comparisons at age 7, test results alone will be used. The fact that no audit will be carried out of TA means, too, that there will be little guarantee of consistency which will also effectively down grade the status of TA.

The fifth innovation in the development of the national assessment programme was the more open *classroom-based style of external test*. The standard assessment task was designed, as its name implies, as a conscious attempt to move away from traditional standardized tests: assessment tasks were to be offered to children which related to a specific primary topic, matched good classroom practice and covered a broad range of activities and response modes. On the basis of these assessment tasks teachers would observe children's performance, question them to gauge their level of understanding and assess written output. Thus the TGAT model emphasized a wide range of response modes in order to minimize the negative effect on the curriculum normally associated with formal assessment. This form of assessment is, however, very time-consuming, and given the requirement for comprehensive coverage, the complexity and load involved resulted in widespread publicity about the amount of time the SATs were taking in 1991. This outcry caused the move to shorter, more standardized paper and pencil procedures for 1992, and to further simplifications in later years.

Thus, the background to this study was one of a major innovation in curriculum linked to an innovatory assessment programme. As well as political anxieties about a new and possibly less rigorous assessment system, there were genuine problems in the development and articulation of the TGAT model: the level of specificity of the assessment criteria, the combination of new types of external tests and teachers' assessments and the relationship of each of these to the national curriculum itself, and the ten-level scale, were all problematic. During the course of the period 1990–93 all these elements were reconsidered and in some cases changed. The picture for primary teachers, then, was one of huge amounts of new material and activities to master, with little training or support, and constantly changing requirements.

National assessment in primary schools: an evaluation

This research study was set up to examine not just the implementation of the national assessment programme, but also whether primary teachers became more sophisticated and knowledgeable in assessment, or whether they simply learned to operate an imposed system. (A full list of publications from this research project is given on page 189.) Was there evidence of the use of TA results to modify the work programmes for individual children – in other words, to use this assessment information formatively? Given the lack of a model for carrying out TA and the limited training in this area, the research aimed to find out how teachers carried out the TA required of them and in what ways this differed from the assessment used prior to the introduction of the national curriculum. We also looked at the impact of the assessment on teachers' practice and attempted to seek indications as to whether standards or expectations were rising as the government and HMI intended.

The research was carried out in 32 schools, eight in each of four LEAs which were chosen to represent different socio-economic and geographic conditions:

- Northshire, a county in North East England with rural areas and towns;
- Homeshire, a county in South East England with rural areas, semi-rural areas and an affluent commuter belt;
- Midboro, a Midlands metropolitan borough with inner-city and industrial areas;
- Innercity, a London borough with high levels of unemployment, a high proportion of non-English-speaking families and poor housing.

We chose these four LEAs specifically to represent different characteristics so that we could observe the introduction of national assessment in as broad a range of settings as possible. Within each LEA we chose eight schools at random, but so as to be representative of the LEA in respect of the school characteristics of size and type (infant, first or primary; Church or maintained), and as far as possible to reflect the socio-economic make-up of the LEA population.

Within each of these 32 schools we focused on one Year 2 teacher as well as interviewing, on regular occasions, the head and other Y2 teachers in the school. In the event, 22 of the classes turned out to be of mixed age and/or team-teaching based, with the remaining ten of the 32 classes containing Y2 children only.

The field work was divided into five phases. Phase 1 (1990–91) involved obtaining information about the schools and the teachers' normal practice, organization of the classroom and previous assessment policy and practice. We then observed the SATs themselves in spring/summer 1991 in 30 of the schools. Following this, we interviewed the heads and the Y2 teachers about the administration of the SATs.

Phase 2 (1991–2) focused on six case-study schools in which Y2 classes were observed and teachers interviewed extensively about their TA practice. At this time we used the 'quote-sort' technique with the case-study teachers (and later with 19 teachers who were still in Y2). By sorting statements about TA collected in phase 1 into 'like me / not like me' teachers were able to describe in much greater detail how they were assessing children's work.

Phase 3 involved detailed observation of selected SATs in spring / summer 1992 in 17 schools where the Y2 teacher was the same as in the previous year. Where no SAT was observed because the Y2 teacher had changed, we interviewed the head to find out about the organization and workload of the SATs for 1992.

Phase 4 took place in summer 1992. Postal questionnaires were sent to Y2 teachers in all the 31 schools remaining in the study (one had dropped out through change of Head) to follow up the assessment experiences in 1992. Parents were also interviewed in the six case-study schools.

Phase 5 took place in autumn 1992 when postal questionnaires about the use of results in 1992 were sent to heads and Y3 teachers in all schools. Heads were asked about the impact of national assessment on their schools and staff over the past three years.

Throughout the five phases of the project LEA staff were interviewed regularly about assessment training, policy and use of results.

A further set of information was collected from October 1993 once a new research project had begun: NAPS 2 built on the work of, and involved some of the schools in, NAPS 1, but is focused mainly on assessment at Key Stage 2. In this phase we asked teachers about their experience of SATs in 1993 and also asked heads for a retrospective view of the impact of the assessment requirements on standards of teaching and learning over the three years.

In 1994 we kept in touch with the eight headteachers and seven continuing Y2 teachers from NAPS 1 and we were able to visit four schools while SATs were in progress. A questionnaire was sent to these seven teachers and also to 21 other Y2 teachers who worked in schools in our new project. In this way we were able to collect information on the changes made to statutory requirements and on how national assessment was developing at Key Stage 1.

In the next chapter we start the presentation of our findings with a chapter on teachers' assessment of children's attainment.

2

TAKING ASSESSMENT FROM MIND TO PAPER: DEVELOPING TEACHER ASSESSMENT

A key focus of our study was teachers' assessment practice. Our aim was to ascertain whether and how teachers were developing skills and understanding in assessment as a result of the imposed national assessment programme. Teachers' own classroom-based informal assessment of children's attainment was thus a key focus, and much of our early fieldwork was devoted to finding out how individual teachers and their schools were planning to carry out this aspect of national assessment.

Teachers were not offered a model of Teacher Assessment (TA) by the Department for Education and they were largely left alone to implement TA with only a minimal input from their LEA advisers (Bennett *et al.* 1992). It is perhaps not surprising, then, that teachers came up with a range of approaches. This chapter describes teachers' developing assessment practices in the first two years of national assessment, and introduces three TA models which we abstracted from our data using a variety of research methods. We should point out that these models were pre-boycott, pre-Dearing Review and pre-curriculum changes; in NAPS 2 we are investigating whether the models hold true post 1992 and with Y6 teachers.

Background

Our initial visits to Y2 teachers were made between January and April 1991 when national assessment was in its first year of implementation. TA was due to be finished by 31 March, with SATs following close behind. We visited all 32 Y2 teachers and had an hour-long interview about national assessment, both TA and SATs. We also observed their classrooms for whole or half days and interviewed headteachers about assessment within the context of the school.

Anxieties about impending SATs were running high and, against this background, TA tended to take a back seat. It is clear from some of the interviews that, while we were asking about TA, the teachers were responding in terms of SATs. For teachers, SATs were much more of an issue than TA, even in the early visits before TA had been started. Teachers saw the 'examness' of SATs as being more important, and therefore more worrying, than their TA; we found the same feature with Y6 teachers in 1994, the year of the Key Stage 2 Pilot tests.

Articulating teacher assessment

One of the major problems we faced in the first interviews was getting teachers to articulate how they would do, or had done, their TA. Many of the interviews yielded vague descriptions of collecting evidence and details of record-keeping and planning:

> I keep a folder for each child with pieces of work, a bit of this, a bit of that, as you go along.

> I looked at my notebook, my lists, the children's books and exercise books. From that I could work out their level.

> I'll spread out all their records and get my stuff and go through it.

Teachers found it difficult to describe precisely what they used to determine levels of attainment, and how they reached this decision. Even where teachers claimed that they used 'attainment targets', by which they usually meant the statements of attainment (SoAs) within the attainment targets, it was not clear how they had done so. One teacher's method of assessing English, for example, was to look at two or three exercise books from each child, 'refer to the attainment target' and assign a level.

When asked, ten teachers were able to describe their TA practice in some detail on science AT1, although not all of these were able to articulate how they decided on a level to record for a particular child. Teachers who were most systematic in their approach to TA were best able to articulate their methods.

The main focus of schools in the first half of the spring term of 1991 was on devising and introducing a system of record-keeping for national curriculum assessment. Much effort had been put into the design of record sheets which would allow Y2 teachers to record national curriculum attainment at Key Stage 1. This focus on record-keeping was, for many schools, the first step towards addressing national assessment, and an introduction to the idea of criterion referencing – that is, assessing against the SoAs.

Some schools had started work on their record sheets up to two years previously and had trialled, or were in the process of trialling, the sheets, not always for the first time. Some schools were still struggling with their sheets, or were finding their recording system cumbersome or unworkable. A few schools had developed or were developing a whole-school assessment policy. Some intended to use their record sheets to pass up through the whole school and were involving all teachers in the recording discussion. In others, however, assessment was strictly a Y2 event, and the Y2 teacher worked alone, with some help from the headteacher.

Records tended to be about coverage of topics, with elaborate systems of ticks, triangles, coloured boxes, etc., to indicate varying degrees of 'visiting' (coverage of a topic), 'understanding' or 'attaining' or 'know/use/understand'. In common with the findings of NFER/BGC (1991), we observed that many schools had elaborate record-keeping systems based on statements of attainment (although it was clear that they did not always use SoAs, as discussed later). In schools where SoAs were not included in the records Y2 teachers felt they were at a disadvantage. Some teachers within the same schools met together to interpret the SoAs and break them down into what they viewed as more manageable 'can do' lists.

The intense focus on record-keeping in 1991 acted as something of a diversion from the need to get to grips with national assessment in its first year. Levels of awareness about TA differed considerably among our 32 teachers. Some accepted assessment as a legal requirement: 'We are all resigned that we've got to do it.' There was a sense that assessment's time had come and it could no longer be ignored, as it had been in the past:

> We have just been jogging along about assessment, filling these in, talking about it, but this term we have got to get it on to paper. By March we have to have it in place.

There were links made to the professionalism and accountability of teachers, with the implication that national assessment had been brought in because 'some teachers were not teaching to a reasonable standard' or working hard enough:

> All assessment is really about is an outcry about teachers . . . 'Let's make the buggers work.'

Some, however, welcomed the new 'accountability' and the idea that national assessment 'will pick out [teachers] who need extra help'.

Although most of our 32 teachers had done something towards TA at the time of our visit, nine had done no recording towards TA and at least four of these had done nothing at all. While some teachers complained that LEA INSET was coming too little and too late, these nine teachers appeared to be postponing their TA as long as they could, waiting either for training, further inspiration, or the deadline of 31 March. Not surprisingly, these teachers found it impossible to describe how they would do their TA when the time came; they simply had no idea.

The most extreme examples of postponing TA were in the London inner-city schools, where INSET came late (as late as the middle of February for one school). In four schools from the same LEA, Y2 teachers trusted that TA could be done by relying on the Primary Language Record (PLR). While the PLR contains general comments on children's abilities in reading, writing and speaking, it was not related to the specific SoAs of English in the national curriculum. The Primary *Learning* Record (PLER) is a post-national curriculum extension of the PLR, relating to levels and ATs in mathematics and science; the schools mentioned above were not using this. However, headteachers in schools which used the PLR clearly valued it and saw it as contributing to national assessment, and had given this message to their teachers, some of whom were worried about doing their TA in so little time. This contrasts sharply with three other schools from the same LEA, where teachers were clearly not postponing TA.

It was clear in 1991 that infant and primary schools were phasing out the use of standardized tests in favour of national assessment. Two of our LEAs were still requiring tests (Young's Reading Test and the LEA Screening Test), but teachers did not find these tests useful and did not feel that they would contribute to national assessment. Nine schools still continued using standardized tests not required by their LEA. Most of this testing was done with a lack of enthusiasm ('grave reservations') and even a lack of confidence that it was the 'right' test to be doing. Standardized testing was sometimes done on the basis that is was 'better than nothing', or for 'a quick overall picture and comparison of reading scores'. Many schools had reviewed or were reviewing their use of standardized tests in view of the work involved in national assessment.

HMI (1991) stated that good practice in assessment could be brought about by a balanced combination of methods. In 1991 many of our Y2 teachers, in preparation for TA, began to do three things:

- collect evidence of children's work which they would save as proof including such things as photographs (especially in science) and tape recordings of reading;
- use observation (especially in maths and science) as a technique of assessment;
- record the information.

In particular, some teachers took detailed notes of their observations, questioned children closely to determine understanding, and planned assessment into their teaching.

Bennett *et al.* (1992) found that of the 114 Y2 teachers in their sample who carried out assessment in 1991, 61% claimed to have acquired some knowledge about assessment techniques over the period of implementing their TA. The source of this knowledge was not always LEA training, although 58% had some training in collecting evidence of attainment, 56% in completing records for TA and 56% in observing children.

Collecting evidence

Our teachers were beginning to consider the collection of evidence in relation to national assessment, and to collect children's work in both systematic and unsystematic ways. They were realizing that 'evidence does not all have to be written' and 'for some ATs it's a lot of observation and you have to ask them what they've done because it's processes'.

Overall, teachers were beginning to collect a wider range of evidence than they had before, including photographs and tape recordings; not just relying on 'tangible' products such as pieces of work, notes children made on paper, work in exercise books and summative tests. Photographs tended to be thought of as evidence where 'tangible' written work was not available:

> Photos can show an outcome of work or can be used to show a child's approach, for example to model making. They can almost become a diary of primary school days.

Collecting children's work was something most teachers had done previously, although they had not previously collected it specifically as evidence of attainment. Children's work tended to be collected haphazardly, and in some cases teachers were saving all the work children did with the intention that some of the work would serve as evidence:

> I keep every scrap of work until I've committed myself to paper.

It is likely that teachers who collected work unsystematically and saved all of it were doing so because they were not yet confident of national assessment criteria and did not know which of the work they would need, or how they would assess it. On the other hand, we found that some teachers were keeping a 'small, carefully selected range of work' as was later suggested by SEAC (1991a). In our sample, eleven teachers were now collecting children's work in a systematic way, in other words, specifically and purposefully in relation to assessment. Collected samples of children's work were in some cases matched to SoAs, with the SoA written on the work itself.

Many teachers realized that different subject areas could require different kinds of evidence:

Not all my TA draws upon the same type of information. Most of it is ongoing in English and maths as certain skills and understanding are mastered. Science assessments have been derived more from specific tasks.

Teachers found assessing some subjects more difficult than others. The Consortium for Assessment and Testing in Schools (1990) had found that teachers were more comfortable with assessing English than with assessing maths or science. Science AT1 was the hardest of all ATs to assess: 58% of teachers in the NFER/BGC (1991) study rated this AT 'hard or fairly hard' to assess. Ten of our teachers corroborated this evidence, calling science AT1 'terribly difficult' and 'a real headache':

> I feel less confident in assessing maths and science, especially science. I don't feel the same confidence that I feel in assessing reading.

Science AT1 was found to be difficult because 'it [was] processes', which were felt by teachers to be more difficult to assess than outcomes. For those who preferred written evidence, the other problem was that science tended not to yield children's written work as evidence. Speaking and listening, the other 'process'-based AT, was found to be the most difficult within English 'because it's not so much a skill, it's more how they behave'. English was found to be easiest to assess because 'written work is obvious evidence' and because 'you know what they can cope with, they are doing it all the time'. Knowing the children was seen to be important and valid evidence in English: 'When you talk to them you *know*'.

Assessing maths was seen by most teachers to be relatively easy because 'the written evidence is there for each child' and attainment is clearer to determine: 'they can or they can't'.

Observing

One of the important new ways of gathering evidence, as most teachers were finding, was the use of observation, particularly in science. This is corroborated by the Primary Assessment, Curriculum and Experience Project which found that observation of individuals and groups was a major area of innovation in assessment practice

(Broadfoot *et al.* 1991). The idea of observing children was not new to teachers, who had done observations of children during their training, although not in relation to assessment. Observation as a technique was therefore familiar, and many teachers were comfortable with it.

Twenty-one Y2 teachers in our sample mentioned observation as a method of assessing children:

> I found the value of having time out to observe children: I found that very useful. I do more of that, I stand back and observe.

> . . . real observation. You really do observe the children and assess the tasks they are doing.

Talking to children was also often claimed by teachers to be a useful method of assessing them. HMI (1991) said that 'good teachers recognised the importance of individual questioning to check children's understanding':

> A lot of assessment used to be a gut feeling but now I find I am going back and checking. I'm observing children far more thoroughly and doing more talking with them.

> In my diary I put a small list of questions I will ask each child in order to check their knowledge.

> Samples of work are not evidence in themselves. You have to ask a child questions about a month later.

Despite the widespread use of observation in Y2 classrooms, it was clear that many of these teachers were observing children in a general way, rather than specifically in relation to SoAs. Only four teachers were observing children against a list based on SoAs. Nevertheless, the familiarity of observation from teacher training may have enabled teachers to take the first step in the gradual shift from summative to formative assessment.

Note-taking and writing down

Most schools had made a move towards more systematic record-keeping, usually in an attempt to address national curriculum coverage. Twenty teachers reported that they were recording assessment in a more systematic way, and some had found this to be an advantage, particularly the 'focusing in on each child':

'It's very easy to miss children and this way is much more foolproof – showing you've talked to a child.

[Assessment] focuses the mind. You *do* concentrate, you *don't* leave people out. You don't assume things.

There is a lot more written down. You have to focus on certain things. You have to do it. Before people may have let it ride and you forget.

It was common for teachers, even prior to national assessment, to keep notes of 'significant breakthroughs' made by children during the year (for instance, when a child who is normally silent speaks up in the context of a small group). However, such records quite often provided only partial information about children's achievements (Clift *et al.* 1981). As a result of TA, particularly observation, many teachers were finding the need to make written notes of what they had observed, or of what children had said. Eighteen teachers said that they made notes to refer to later, or what one teacher called 'taking assessment from mind to paper':

The major change in my assessment has been the need to write things down, which before I would have kept in my head.

I would never have kept that notebook. That's because I have to fill in that assessment sheet.

Some teachers admitted that they found observation 'quite hard work' and that it was difficult to sit back and watch without teaching. Five teachers mentioned particular difficulties with observation: mainly the practical implications of recording or making written notes at the same time as observing children. Some also worried about the effect their note-taking would have on the children. One teacher had practised note-taking in front of the children 'to get them used to it'.

Planning assessment

One approach was purposely to avoid planning assessment in, but to look for 'assessment opportunities' as they arose:

> You observe things and make a note of things that just happen. You think 'Oh! That's another AT'. You make a note of these things and at the end of the day you put them into your records where relevant.

> I'm trying hard to do what I've always done. The way I approach assessment is to do the work I plan to do and then see what ATs can be matched to it.

The avoidance of planned assessment was seen by some teachers to be less 'interfering' with their normal practice, and less intrusive on the children; it also had the advantage of requiring little change to classroom practice.

On the other hand, six teachers described how they were building assessment into their planning: One teacher described her system of planning assessment into her half-term forecast, then looking at which AT to cover during the week and which SoAs she would assess. She would then choose which child to assess, when and how, as well as what to do with the other children while she was assessing. Many other teachers were clearly planning with assessment in mind, and 20 teachers had set specific assessment tasks:

> You have to think about the AT and set up the activity to assess that, so you have to plan ahead.

> In order to make some assessment I specifically design relevant tasks, some of a cross-curricular nature, to check children's abilities and knowledge.

Some organizational changes were needed in order to plan for assessment. One teacher described how she targeted five children to assess in 'prime time' on Monday mornings while she has a support teacher present. Two schools were building up a collection of assessment tasks to be shared within the school:

> We as a staff have devised a growing bank of tasks that are most helpful to assess particular ATs, labelled 'This is a Key Stage 1 Assessment Task'.

Criterion referencing

The use of observations, note-taking and planned-in assessment did not necessarily mean that teachers were assessing against criteria in 1991. The NFER found that despite 96% of teachers recording at SoA level, teachers were actually making global summative assessments at AT level which were not based on accumulated SoA-related information (NFER/BGC 1991: 6); in other words, most teachers were not assessing against SoAs in an ongoing way. This was no doubt due to a range of reasons: the teachers did not realize they were supposed to, they had not been shown how to, there were too many SoAs, they were not very useful as a basis for assessment, etc. We discuss this more fully in the last chapter.

Five of our schools had devised a 'can do' list by breaking down SoAs:

> We've broken down ATs into 'can dos' so if children don't get to Level 1 in the AT we have all these bits and pieces to show what they *have* done.

> We've broken down ATs into a 'can do' list and we observe children against this list.

One school used SoAs for ongoing assessment in science AT1 only; the teacher devised an activity appropriate to the children's topic work and observed children against the 'can do' list. Each child was assessed once per term so that by the end of the year the children had been assessed three times on science AT1 and the teacher was then able to assign a level.

Seven additional teachers said they were using SoAs, usually at the time of recording rather than planning, and were assessing against SoAs directly as part of the assessment process. At four schools we saw evidence of the systematic collection of children's work which was marked with SoAs. Two teachers from the same school who did team-teaching kept the SoAs beside them and discussed them continuously, recording in detail on the school record sheets. Overall, therefore, seven teachers (22% of our sample) appeared to be assessing children against SoAs in an ongoing formative way. The remainder were making global summative assessment at AT level rather than against individual SoAs.

Many teachers found the notion underlying criterion referencing difficult, in that it required teachers to ignore factors such as effort, behaviour and social background:

> I try to remain unbiased in my assessment, but I find children's behavioural problems difficult to ignore.

The notion of the 'whole child' and 'separating out what you know about the child' was a major concern:

> You have to look at it objectively and I find it very hard. It's something you have to learn to do because you know the whole child.

> I don't think I will be able to discount what I know about a child from its attainment. No one can tell the effort behind the result as well as the teacher.

While some teachers acknowledged both the difficulties and the necessity in this model of separating out what they knew about the child from its attainment, some teachers clearly felt that was wrong. One teacher felt that evidence 'includes what I know about the child'. Another teacher said she would consult her behavioural records when doing her TA 'because it gives me a sense of the child, their motivation and where they are'.

Making changes for teacher assessment

Many teachers commented on the 'changes in every aspect of how teachers assess'.

> Before, if a teacher was unsure about how to assess a child, it could be left and ignored, but now because it has to be recorded and a parent will respond, a positive response has to be made.

> Everyone is more day-to-day record conscious.

Twelve teachers responded that they had made changes in their practice in order to do TA and were able to describe how they had done, or were doing, their TA in 1991. For these teachers, doing TA involved:

- setting up specific assessment tasks;
- having a systematic means of collecting evidence;

- observing children's work;
- using and interpreting SoAs.

These teachers fit into a category called *mechanical user* by Hord (1987): after orientating and preparing for the innovation, the user makes changes to organize better use of the innovation. Some of these teachers went on to refine their use of assessment and to co-ordinate its use with colleagues, categories which Hord calls respectively *refinement* and *integration*.

Six teachers stated clearly that they had made no changes in their methods of assessment, with some assessing in the way they had always done, using summative tests at the end of a topic or term.

Although one teacher had accommodated observation as a technique, there was a reluctance to trust her observation, so assessment was ultimately based on the worksheet:

> I set up activities and watch them and once I feel they've understood thoroughly what's going on, then I give them a worksheet. After the worksheet I assess the outcome and award a level.

'Postponers' had not done any recording of TA at the time of our visit, although some 'orientation and preparation' (Hord 1987) had been done at one of these schools. (We have used the term 'postponer' rather than Hord's 'non-user' because some visits were towards the beginning of the term and therefore in advance of the 31 March deadline.) It seemed unlikely that those who postponed their TA would make significant changes to accommodate national assessment because of their general reluctance to accept change and their strongly held views about child-centred practice:

> I would never like it to take over from my teaching. Teaching is more important than assessing. I just keep on teaching children, that's what I've been trained for. I fail to see the value of it.

> I use my memory a lot when it comes to recording. I trust my general impression and memory of children's work. That is the way I've always done it.

One of the reasons for not making changes was the strongly held belief that teaching and assessing are incompatible. Two teachers stated this clearly:

You're either teaching or assessing. You can't be doing both.

There is no time to observe, assess and record in the classroom while teaching.

To sum up, it is clear that there were changes in assessment practices for many teachers in 1991. Along with summative tests, children's workbooks and folders of work, a greater variety of evidence was being used by most teachers and observation as a technique became more widely used in general, sometimes accompanied by on-the-spot note-taking. More systematic record-keeping was being done in most schools and assessment was being planned in, usually by linking ATs to topic work. Despite these changes, SoAs were not used to make assessments by most teachers. NFER/BGC (1991) found that one in eight teachers had made their judgements for TA without using any recorded evidence and recommended that more emphasis needed to be placed on making judgements against SoAs, rather than globally. Many of our teachers confirmed this 'it's just a feeling of what they can do' approach to TA in 1991.

Towards a model of teacher assessment: the quote-sort method

Despite the amount of evidence described in this chapter, by the end of our first phase of fieldwork in 1991, we felt that we had little understanding of, or feel for, how teachers took their assessments from mind to paper. Collecting examples of work was the most popular approach, but this in itself does not explain how the process of collecting evidence works as an assessment device. We decided, therefore, to develop in 1992 a more specific way of eliciting this information: this involved a sorting activity based on quotations about TA which were selected from those made by teachers in our 1991 interviews. This method involved asking teachers to sort 16 quotes (Table 2) into 'like me' or 'not like me' categories. After the teachers had sorted the quotes we had a detailed interview, asking each of them to explain the reasons behind the sorting, thus allowing us to combine both qualitative and quantitative methods. Altogether, 25 Y2 teachers were involved: seven from the six case-study schools (one school had a pair of teachers working as a team)

Table 2 Teachers' quotes

		Number of teachers agreeing out of 25
A	I try to remain unbiased in my assessments but I find children's behavioural problems difficult to ignore.	14
B	We have broken down ATs into a 'can do' list and we observe children against this list.	5
C	There is a lot of oral work in science and I find you can assess English skills through science activities even though the emphasis is on science.	24
D	I don't think I will be able to discount what I know about the child from its attainment. No one can tell the effort behind the result as well as the teacher.	11
E	I look at how it all went, how children approached the task, their attitude, whether they were copying or following the leader, whether they attained or covered.	24
F	For a lot of ATs you can use written work. For some it's a lot of observation and you have to ask them what they've done because it's processes.	25
G	From our maths scheme you can hang quite a lot on the ATs, so I would use those worksheets and I can tell quite a lot through the worksheets.	12
H	I set up activities and watch them and once I feel they've understood thoroughly, then I give them a worksheet. After the worksheet I assess the outcome and award a level.	13
I	You observe things and make a note of things that just happen. You think 'Oh, that's another AT'. You make a note of these things and at the end of the day you put them into your records where relevant.	10
J	At the end of each term or half term I call up my memory of a child's performance on the AT.	8

Table 2   (contd)

		Number of teachers agreeing out of 25
K	I do a lot of talking to the children to see if they exhibit the sort of knowledge that you think fits the AT.	24
L	I feel that recording at the time is more accurate than reflecting back.	15
M	I look at an SoA and devise a small list of questions which will test a child's knowledge of that SoA. I put the list into my diary and, during the activity, ask all the children in the group the same set of questions.	10
N	I take a photograph either as a record of work done, like when a child has made a model, or as a trigger to my own memory. The snap triggers my memory back to the questions children were asking or the knowledge they were displaying or the way they were going about something, like on a field trip when the children are involved and enjoying something.	11
O	I keep a piece of paper with me with the ATs and SoAs clearly written out.	5
P	You are either teaching or assessing; you can't be doing both.	4

and 18 from the non-case-study schools (selecting only those in which the Y2 teacher had not changed between 1991 and 1992).

Although there were some minor difficulties in using authentic quotes (such as confusion resulting from negatives in the wording and the inclusion of more than one idea within the same quote), the teachers engaged with the activity very positively because they felt the quotes were 'real'. The data from the quote-sort activity and the detailed diagnostic interview was analysed at several levels (see Table 3 for details). As a result of this, we identified three models or 'ideal types' of teacher assessment, which differ according to:

• how systematic they are;
• whether they integrate assessment into teaching;
• what kind of ideas about teaching and learning lie behind them.

Table 3 Developing the models of teacher assessment

1 Interview and observation data gathered from all 32 schools.

2 SATs visits to all 32 schools, in which we asked teachers to reflect on their TA and their judgements about individual children.

3 Analysed data from first and second interviews and gathered all teacher quotes about TA. Selected 16 quotes representing different aspects of TA.

4 Selected six case-study schools based on random stratified sample, also representing a variety of observable assessment practices and attitudes, as expressed in the quotes.

5 Gathered data in case-study schools during four day visits:
   • in-depth classroom observation;
   • interviews about planning;
   • account interviews of deciding final levels for individual children;
   • quote-sort activity.

6 Visited 18 non-case-study schools to do the quote-sort activity with a larger sample.

7 Analysed data from the quote-sort activity and carried out a cluster analysis of teachers who are most and least like each other in attitude.

8 Went back to observation data to group teachers according to TA behaviour.

9 Combined attitudes and behaviour to form first tentative categories for models.

10 Placed teachers within categories according to attitude and behaviour data available.

11 Refined models and gave them names based on characteristics they represent. Reconsidered the placement of some teachers.

12 Validated models by sending them out to Y2 teachers as vignettes (Table 4).

The models are not hierarchical in value and no particular set of views or practices is intended to represent a desired model of teacher assessment, although the systematic planners were the only group assessing against SoAs in the way encouraged by SEAC. Indeed, our informal judgement suggests that there were teachers within each of the models whose pupils had both relatively high and relatively low standards of attainment.

The first tentative models were refined several times by the project team. The models emerged from the analysis of *all* the data gathered from Y2 teachers during the first two phases of the project (interviews, classroom observation, quote-sort activity and related interview, review of records and record-keeping practices, accounts of curriculum planning and detailed descriptions of how levels were arrived at for one child). The detailed observation of case-study teachers was especially helpful in fleshing out the details.

The models of teacher assessment

The three models of TA distinguish *intuitives*, *evidence gatherers* and *systematic planners*. These names were chosen by the team to represent what we felt to be the best summary of the characteristics of each group. They are described below.

Intuitives

For these teachers, assessment is a kind of 'gut reaction', hence the term 'intuitive'. They clearly rely upon their memory of what children can do and so, during the study, it was difficult for us to observe any ongoing teacher assessment or describe the processes that they were using. They spoke about assessment in general terms, without reference to SoAs in the national curriculum:

> Sitting on my own at night when it's nice and quiet and the children have gone home, I looked through what I had for the child, I called on my memory, plans I had made for what we'd covered, and looked in their folders . . .

The teachers in this group are critical of the imposed system of national assessment. They feel it is disruptive to their usual, mostly intuitive, ways of working with children, and, of all the teachers in the study, intuitives have made the least amount of change to their practice. One of the main characteristics of this group is their rejection of systematic, recorded TA because it interferes with 'real teaching'.

> I just can't bear the thought of breaking off to give them a tick. To be honest, in my classroom, I can't keep breaking off and writing things down.

They further criticize a systematic approach as being too formal and clinical – 'too structured – down such tramlines' – and they show a particular dislike of 'the clipboard syndrome': the idea of going round recording all the time.

Rather, when making their assessments, intuitives rely on an all-round close knowledge of children built up over time. This includes what they know about children's 'everyday performance, personality, the way they present themselves, their acquisition of knowledge outside of school' and the way the children behave in groups. This makes it difficult for the teachers to separate out attainment from all these other things:

> I don't think I can discount what I know about a child from its attainment.

Some, however, believe that these details should, in fact, be included as part of assessment:

> You have to take account of the contextual issues because that's what being a professional is.

Similarly, intuitives often find it hard to ignore children's attitudes and behaviour when recording levels:

> If a child had really tried and put a lot of effort in it, it's very hard not to give it [the national curriculum level] to them

and they may make other allowances:

> It's so unfair – one of the August birthdays is quite a bright little boy. He just hasn't got there yet. So I feel like giving him a little more leeway.

In general, then, intuitives are inclined to include different kinds of biographical and contextual details when making their assessments, and because they find it difficult to 'distil' attainment from all this, one can say that intuitives are passive resisters of the idea of the criterion-referenced system embraced within the national assessment model.

Within this broad group, we were able to identify two distinct subgroups, and have termed them *children's needs ideologists* and *tried and tested practitioners*.

Children's needs ideologists
The teachers in this group show a great deal of confidence in their arguments about children's needs and about how children learn, and can be very articulate in defending a child-centred view of education. Their view of assessment is linked to this. As their curriculum

planning is based on what the teachers feel are the needs of children, there is no need for them to have internalized either attainment targets or statements of attainment because 'you can't always follow what you, *the teacher*, intend to do'. In other words, the teachers would not plan to restrict the content of a day's work to a particular AT or set of SoAs because a child's needs might at any time dictate a particular kind of teaching input or reinforcement.

For these teachers formalized systematic TA is not acceptable. The idea of going round assessing a child systematically against a 'can do' list or graded set of objectives does not fit within the child-centred view of the teacher's role. Tactics like devising a list of questions to ask every child 'ignores what the child is saying back to you' and this kind of negotiation between teacher and child is important in the child-centred philosophy. For these teachers, an essential part of teaching is ongoing interaction with the child, and if you are a non-participant note-taker, you cannot do this – it is 'too hard to sit back and let a child struggle' without offering some input because 'as a teacher it is second nature' to do this. Focused note-taking may even be seen as damaging because children 'are left alone and their concentration breaks down'.

For assessment purposes, children's needs ideologists prefer a 'whole approach', seeing teaching and assessing taking place simultaneously. They are 'recording mentally all the time while watching the processes a child is going through'. Children are seen as individuals and teachers may hold individual conferences with children as part of the assessment process, logging the conversations in their heads for subsequent reflection.

Children's needs ideologists tend to hold their own implicit ideas of 'levelness', and may be using these as a basis for TA. The SAT tasks do not always match up to these intuitive notions of the levels:

That was no way a level 3 task. You have to do more to get a level 3. We know what quality work is.

Tried and tested practitioners
We have used this name for this group of intuitives because they continue to use and feel secure with methods of assessment used before the Education Reform Act. However, they do not always explain clearly the reasons for their choices.

For this group, the stress is very much on *teaching*, and the teacher is the one who defines the child's needs and provides the appropriate instruction. The child responds and the teacher marks and gives feedback. Assessment, then, tends to be summative and takes the form of giving home-made tests or worksheets at the end of a lesson or topic, giving worksheets related to published schemes, scrutinizing pages of marked work in exercise books, and testing a child's knowledge after a lesson by 'getting them on their own and having a little chat about it'. The results of these forms of assessment do not relate to the SoAs which form the basis for TA under the national curriculum and are not necessarily analysed or recorded at the time. In fact, tried and tested practitioners reject the idea of ongoing recorded TA because that would mean a radical change to their well-tried ways of working and because they believe that:

you are *either* teaching *or* assessing, you can't be doing both.

At the end of half terms or terms, they call up their memory and feel that:

if you're worth the name of teacher, you should know your children inside out and be able to recall what they can do.

Close knowledge of children is again quoted as the main basis of TA and there is strong feeling that 'the assessing needs to be done by the actual class teacher' in order to decide whether 'what they have done on paper is really amazing for that child'. The implication here is that pieces of children's work cannot be objectively assessed against a set of criteria such as the SoAs.

When it came to SATs, the tried and tested practitioners seemed prepared to carry them out to the letter of the law. This could have been because the SAT materials and instructions were provided for them and giving summative tests was familiar in terms of their own practice.

Evidence gatherers

The second group of teachers we called 'evidence gatherers'. 'Trying to get as much evidence as I can' is the aim of many of these teachers, one of whom described herself as 'a hoarder' who 'keeps everything'.

Evidence may be collected from a variety of sources, including pages from workbooks, worksheets from published schemes, teacher-devised worksheets, children's written work, spelling tests, and notes from questioning children on the work they have done. Evidence gatherers particularly like written evidence: 'getting the result down on paper' is seen to be essential, because teachers feel accountable and, under national assessment, are concerned that they may be asked to produce evidence of their assessments of children:

> I keep a camera in the cupboard for technology. It is the only record you've got if somebody asked you for evidence.

Most evidence gatherers, however, recognize that 'you don't always have a piece of recorded work every time' and that other kinds of evidence, including teacher's notes on observations, may be valid evidence in themselves:

> I set up activities and watch them and then we work on worksheets as well to see what they've done. But the outcome is not just the worksheet, I have assessed the whole process.

One of the evidence gatherer's main concerns, then, is that there must be clear evidence of children's attainment in the national curriculum and that it is the teacher's duty to ensure that such evidence exists:

> I would never rely all on my memory. You must have it backed up with evidence. You've got to keep your notes as evidence.

Evidence gatherers use published schemes of work as evidence but tend not to trust them entirely. There was a fear that such schemes 'miss things out' or fail to cover the national curriculum 'adequately or entirely'. Teachers, therefore, devise their own worksheets to complement the published schemes.

Evidence gathering is associated with a belief that pupils generally learn what is taught and only what is taught; thus, assessment follows teaching in order to check that the process is going according to plan. Overall, a programme of planned topic work is seen to ensure that both national assessment and the national curriculum are being done. The teacher can identify 'gaps' in the curriculum at the time she records on her assessment record sheets, which is usually done termly in the school holidays:

> When you go through and fill in the record sheets you can look at them and just find a little point that you haven't covered, so you make a little note that you have to do this.

With the evidence gathering method, assessment is summative, rather than formative in nature; in other words, as one teacher put it:

> I would just write it down but I wouldn't go into my records until I am ready to record. I leave assessing to the end of term.

At the end of term, 'bits and bobs of evidence' are 'pulled together' and the teacher reflects on the work the child has done over the term:

> If I have their pieces of work there, I can just sit there and think 'this particular child has achieved that'.

Most evidence gatherers prefer not to rely on memory because:

> You just couldn't possibly call up your memory on each child's performance on every AT – it's just too difficult.

However, with large amounts of evidence that has been collected available at the time of recording, it is unlikely that all the evidence will be used in the awarding of levels.

One of the main characteristics of evidence gatherers is that assessment is accommodated within the teacher's existing ways of working and is not always planned in. Rather than planning specifically for assessment, evidence gatherers tend to rely on 'assessment opportunities' to arise within their normal classroom teaching:

> I don't really plan a task to cover assessment. I plan first what I want to do and then see how it can be fitted into assessment.

Collecting evidence in this way is dependent on the teacher's ability to recognize tasks which can be 'matched' to the national assessment ATs, and to 'vaguely have assessment in mind all the time'. Having recognized an activity as usable for assessment, the teacher then devises a means of gathering evidence:

> A piece of work we did on autumn days, we got to talking about that and a lot of science points came out of it . . . so, quickly do a weather chart! They covered all the other things really well and it was obvious from the discussion, but we just had to have the weather chart for evidence.

Evidence-gathering teachers tend to think in terms of assessing against ATs, rather than SoAs. The 'matching' of tasks to ATs usually takes place after the activity itself, either at the end of the day or at the end of term when recording is done:

> I hadn't really planned how this exercise would fit into assessment, but I see now that it does. I will have to look up exactly where and how it fits in . . . I'll look it up in the book when I get home.

Some evidence gatherers plan in general terms for assessment at the same time as they plan their topic work, usually before each term.

Once topics are chosen, attainment targets are matched against them so that there is a general confidence that national assessment is being 'covered' within the topic work:

> I know that if we cover these topics we'll have done all the ATs. I like things done as part of topic work.

The link between assessment and topic work enables teachers to incorporate assessment into their usual way of doing things, and makes assessment more user-friendly. This means that national assessment can be addressed in such a way that it does not become the 'be-all and end-all' by changing or interfering with normal teaching practice.

Systematic planners

We have called the third group of teachers 'systematic planners' because they plan for assessment on a systematic basis and this has become part of their practice. This means that the teachers consciously devote some part of the school week to assessing:

> I need to know that at a particular time of day, I am actually going to be assessing one thing. You've got to be structured, you've got to know what you are looking for.

They believe strongly in doing ongoing formative assessment which usually involves note-taking at the time:

> The greatest thing is to make notes so that it informs your teaching.

At one school, they have developed a method of instant annotation by attaching the notes directly to the pieces of work:

> We keep boxes of sticky labels at our sides during most activities and we record as we go along or at the end of a session.

For systematic planners, relying solely on memory is thought to be untrustworthy:

> I don't think memory is accurate enough. I think that's when you assume things about children.

The teachers in this group prefer to use many and varied assessment techniques and are keen to fit the assessment technique to the activity being assessed. In the study, we observed them assessing the children formatively both during the day (through planned observation, open-ended questioning, teacher–pupil discussion, running records and serendipitously unplanned observations) and at the end of the week or session (through scrutiny of classwork, notes of critical incidents, annotated pieces of work, annotated photographs and self-designed worksheets). For systematic planners assessment is formative. In other words, assessment is a kind of diagnosis according to how the child is doing on the tasks set, and the teacher takes note and plans accordingly for the next activity:

> You're making some assessment of previous work because you have to assess in order to teach . . . whether they are ready to go on to the next stage.

In systematic planners' classrooms, records are generally accessible and used. These teachers have focused sharply on using the SoAs. In some cases they have broken them down into smaller steps or 'can do' lists which represent the teachers' interpretation of what the statements mean and which spell out what a child might say or do to demonstrate attainment:

> Even with the SoAs, there are still smaller steps. Like, the statement says 'know number facts to 10'. But the steps before that in basic addition . . . there are all sorts of ways of doing that.

Teachers may plan to assess more than one statement at a time, perhaps 'a process one and a content one'. They may also assess the statements several times or 'do a quick stock-take' to be able 'to really say if they have attained it', 'not to push and give a false picture' and to 'double-check, be fair'.

One piece of tangible evidence (particularly work from one published workcard) or one session of observation is thought to be insufficient evidence of attainment because:

> you're teaching to the worksheet, you could be missing out chunks. That's not developing the children.

Through focusing on the criteria, systematic planners have become very familiar with the national assessment procedures and have either internalized the ATs and SoAs, or have them permanently displayed for easy reference (for example, on planning sheets or assessment tick sheets they have made). They can often quote them or recognize attainment when scrutinizing work:

> I think when I'm marking, say, English 3 . . . it leaps up from the page; ah, this is a level 2.

Here we see that it is the children's *work* which is being assessed against the criteria, and the teachers tend not to hold implicit notions of such things as, for example, 'a level 2 *child*'. We have found that they are often willing to try assessing children on higher levels without necessarily teaching the content first. In so doing, assessment seems less bolted on to teaching and becomes a learning process for the teachers themselves:

> The interesting thing about teacher assessments is that they surprise you.

The teachers in this group are able to distil children's attainment in the national curriculum from all the other information they have about them and often record attainment on one type of record and attitudinal, contextual and biographical data on a different type:

> You must be quite specific about what a child has attained. The effort goes into their record of achievement. You make notes of it in other places but not in teacher assessment.

> When a particularly difficult child was being teacher-assessed, the teacher might have been thinking about his general problems in the classroom. We've found that using the criteria, this child, being assessed on exactly the same thing as everyone else, has actually shown he's doing quite well.

Systematic planners may, however, use what they know about a child in planning for assessment or in choosing a particular technique:

> I use my knowledge of the child in my *approach* to teaching and assessing but not in my actual assessment.

When it comes to using all the data from teacher assessment to give children levels:

> The record would be a drawing together of everything.

Within the broad category of systematic planners, there are two identifiable subgroups. Although both subgroups are systematic planners, the *systematic integrators* have changed their daily work patterns to a lesser degree than the *systematic assessors*.

Systematic assessors
These teachers give daily concentrated time to assessing one group of children at a time. They will know in advance which SoAs they will assess and which technique they will use. They will often have pre-

pared 'can do' lists and tick sheets to aid the recording of their ongoing assessments or will use something like the sticky label technique. Later they will read through these sheets and the observation notes as the basis for planning work for those children for the next day.

Some systematic assessors have devised systems to lessen demands made on them by the rest of the class. Certain teachers, for example, wear badges or put up a 'busy' flag as a sign that they are not to be interrupted. Others write out a list of tasks for the children to work through. At the same time, they make it clear to the children that it is quite permissible to ask classmates for help, so as not to distract the teacher.

Systematic integrators

This other subgroup do not separate themselves off from the rest of the class for assessment periods, but circulate, gathering evidence in different ways, which feeds into weekly recorded assessments and informs weekly planning. The clearest example of this occurs in the case of two teachers working as a pair and sharing responsibility for 60 children. They collect assessment data on children throughout the week and meet on Fridays when they consider the data and interpret each other's comments. They then record, on a 'Friday sheet', their jointly agreed assessments of groups of children together with a plan for the next week's work. These two teachers have more or less memorized the SoAs, but keep the national curriculum documents available for consultation. They do not plan to assess a particular group during their teaching time or (except when doing the PLR) make running notes. But, as they go about their teaching, they do collect assessment data in the following ways:

- While doing the PLR, they make notes of a child's reading behaviour and, on the basis of this, write down what they plan to give the child to do next.
- Based on previous assessments, a child may be working on a specifically designed task which targets a particular SoA – the teachers question the child while working. Sometimes on the spot, sometimes after the session, they annotate the piece of work using the child's own words and their own remarks as evidence of achievement of the SoA.
- If the child demonstrates an understanding of a particular AT which is not necessarily being targeted, the teachers hold this 'breakthrough' in their memory until the end of the day.

- They mark writing on the spot, assessing and mentally noting a child's grasp of, for example, capitals and full stops.
- They record contextual factors (like a child's attitude to work) which they feel have affected performance. Tasks or work in some ATs may have to be repeated. This is why the teachers do not do systematic one-off planned assessments in teaching time.
- They record a child's achievement against a checklist of process skills such as 'observing' and 'posing questions'.
- Every day after work they discuss how the children had worked, checking pieces of work together and deciding whether children need further work, enrichment or revision. Based on all this information, they fill in their own reflection sheets every Friday, consulting SoAs again at this point and awarding any levels achieved.
- They photocopy Friday sheets and exchange them with each other, and then plan next week's work.

Comparisons between the models of teacher assessment

Evidence gatherers, on the whole, understand that for national assessment they should distinguish attainment from other contextual factors such as effort and behaviour. Like intuitives, however, some evidence gatherers do not agree with making this distinction. Some evidence gatherers feel that although attainment is clearly separate from other factors ('effort does not equal attainment'), the new assessment procedures require the teacher to suppress what she knows about the 'whole child'. It appears that while evidence gatherers are becoming aware of the theory behind criterion referencing, there are times when contextual factors must be taken into account. In contrast, systematic planners have accepted the criterion-referenced model. They use SoAs as the focus of their planning, whether on a daily or a weekly basis. In some schools the teachers have agreed on the kinds of things they are looking for as evidence of attainment and keep these 'can do' lists to hand for reference. They often decide together which questions will best elicit proof of understanding from children.

A feature of both the intuitive model and most evidence gatherers is that systematic assessment is seen as a threat to relationships with children: most intuitives and some evidence gatherers rejected such systematic practices as note-taking on the spot. The teachers in these two groups, unlike systematic planners, had a fear of national assessment interfering with their relationships with children if they were to 'go over the top' by adopting more systematic assessment practices. Assessing against a 'can do' list was seen as 'tabulated' and 'judgemental', as well as unnecessarily systematic: keeping a list of the ATs and SoAs and referring to them regularly was generally regarded by both evidence gatherers and intuitives as interfering with the 'real job' of teaching. Similarly, recording or note-taking on the spot was seen sceptically, acceptable only 'providing you just jot it down and don't make a thing of it'. While some teachers acknowledged that recording on the spot was more accurate than reflecting back, they did not see it as a priority and had not incorporated it into their own assessment practice.

Overall, evidence gatherers shared concerns with their intuitive colleagues in rejecting the methods of systematic planners. While intuitives were content to rely on memory and intuition for assessment, evidence gatherers favoured gathering evidence and then reflecting back over the child's performance during the term in a summative manner. Systematic planners, on the other hand, assessed groups of children daily or weekly in order to plan subsequent work.

Validating the models

As the three models of teacher assessment arose from our analysis of the data we had gathered, we thought it important to find out to what extent they matched the experience of real teachers and educators. A first validation of the models was carried out by presentation to a group of LEA advisers, who were not from the LEAs in the NAPS sample. The three models were widely recognized and endorsed. Later, other groups of teachers, researchers and LEA personnel also reacted positively. We then presented the models in the form of vignettes (Table 4) to our full sample of Y2 teachers. Teachers were asked to choose the vignette which most closely matched their own practice in order to establish to what extent the descriptions matched their own perceptions. Vignettes seemed an appropriate format to feed back to teachers, as they enabled us to present the essentials of each model, including both behaviour and philosophy, in everyday language with which teachers could identify. They also had the advantage of being brief, which would contribute to the likelihood of response. However, it was difficult to try to capture

Table 4　The vignettes

Model A　*Evidence Gatherer*

I prefer to plan the ATs into my topic work and I know that if we cover these topics we'll have done all the ATs. I tend not to plan too many assessment activities because I think one can become too systematic about assessment. I'm quite familiar with the ATs now, which helps me recognize opportunities for assessment.

I think it's very important to gather as much evidence as I can, things like pieces of children's work, worksheets they've done, little notes I have made, anything I have noticed while they are working.

I do my recording at the half term or the end of term when I sit down with all the evidence I have gathered and think about the child's performance. I wouldn't just rely on my memory for that, you have to have it backed up by evidence. I can give them a level using the evidence plus what I remember.

Overall, I prefer to go about my usual teaching and use assessment opportunities as they occur.

Model B　*Intuitive*

I tend to see assessment as a whole process; it's a part of what teachers do all the time and there is no need to plan it in. I have a general picture of the whole child and what a child can do; this is where the teacher's skills and experience are important.

I prefer assessment to be informal so that spontaneity is not lost. I plan what the children need. I don't have particular ATs or SoAs in mind. I'm recording mentally all the time when watching the processes a child is going through, I don't take notes because I think that can interfere with your relationships with children. I might give a worksheet or a little test to check understanding of something I have taught.

As a professional, I think you have to take account of the contextual issues such as attitudes and social background.

When it comes to recording for national assessment, I can reflect on what I know about the child.

Model C　*Systematic Planner*

I need to know that at a particular time of day I am actually going to be assessing. I like to be structured and know which SoAs I want to assess. Beforehand, I try to interpret the SoAs and break them down into a kind of 'can do' list: descriptions of what children might do or say to show they are meeting the national curriculum criteria. I may assess the same SoA more than once, to double-check and be fair.

I'll observe and question the children while they are working and record at the time or soon afterwards on my own checklists. These notes will inform my future planning because you have to assess in order to teach.

I think you need to be quite specific about what a child has attained on the national curriculum and record this separately from other things like effort, context and background details; they can be recorded elsewhere, say in a child's record of achievement.

While observing, I am often surprised by what children can do (especially in areas I haven't yet taught) and overall I feel that doing ongoing TA has improved my skills as a teacher.

essential features *and* to differentiate between the different types. Nevertheless, no teacher gave us feedback that the models were unrealistic or that it was difficult to choose one to identify with. Seven teachers did not return a vignette for reasons apparently unconnected with the task, such as resignation, retirement or school closure.

Response to the vignettes was requested from all Y2 teachers in our sample schools, now down to 31. Altogether 31 Y2 teachers from 24 schools responded to the vignettes. They placed themselves within the models as follows:

Model A (evidence gatherers)	14
Model B (intuitives)	6
Model C (systematic planners)	10
Parts of model A and model C	1
Unable to say	0

These responses to the vignettes provided a partial validation of the teacher assessment models in the sense that 31 teachers were prepared to commit themselves to a model, thereby recognizing and being able to identify with the models in practice.

Of these 31 teachers, 19 were our original Y2 teachers and so familiar to us. Of the 19 teachers (who did both the quote-sort activity and the vignettes) 14 chose the model, or combination of models, which we had felt best matched their practice from the data we had available. The extent of the overlap is further validation of the models; we had not expected a complete match since we were aware that the teachers' perceptions of their assessment practice sometimes would differ from our descriptions of their practice which were based in turn on our own perceptions.

In some cases we identified teachers as between two models and in some of these cases we felt they were moving from one to another. In Chapter 7 we describe what happened as the national curriculum innovation bedded down.

Summary

In the spring of 1991, the main focus for our teachers had been on devising record-keeping systems for the national curriculum. At that time, perceptions of teacher assessment differed considerably, with some teachers seeing it as a legal requirement to call teachers into account and others welcoming this new development and seeing assessing as an important part of teaching. At that time most of our teachers found it difficult to articulate TA and to describe precisely what they were doing to determine children's levels of attainment. For many of them the assessment process itself was intuitive.

Expertise in TA was embryonic and as it developed our teachers tended to concentrate on saving proof of attainment by collecting lots of evidence. A few were, however, beginning to change their assessment practices – trying new techniques such as taking photographs, and doing more close observation of children at work. With these teachers, on-the-spot note-taking was becoming more widespread, but these notes were not necessarily related to the SoAs. Indeed, during 1991 there was very little evidence that teachers were using SoAs as a basis for making criterion-referenced assessments.

As our study progressed, we were able to describe three emerging models of TA. Intuitives, both children's needs ideologists and tried and tested practitioners, had made least change to their usual ways of working. Evidence gatherers had accommodated the new rules within their existing practices by collecting evidence and doing summative assessments at the end of term. Systematic integrators had continued with their day-to-day teaching strategies, but had introduced regular weekly slots for assessment. Those that had made most changes were the systematic assessors, who had changed their teaching routines by deliberately planning in specific daily time for assessment. These teachers, by focusing on SoAs, were beginning to use criterion-referenced approaches. All except the intuitives had moved to more evidence-based and recorded assessments and away from intuitive held-in-the-head assessment.

This chapter has described TA during the first two years of national assessment; there has clearly been an impact on teachers' ways of working. Teacher assessment, however, forms only one part of the national assessment programme. Children are also required to be assessed by standard assessment tasks. How teachers managed and reacted to these tests is the focus of the next chapter.

3

SATs: THE OBJECTIVE EVIDENCE?

The SATs for seven-year-olds in 1991 were mostly activity-based tasks, described in Chapter 1 as 'performance assessment', which had to be given individually or in small groups by the class teacher. The national assessment programme, as outlined in the TGAT report (DES 1988), was to have two strands: external tests and TA. The tests, called Standard Assessment Tasks, were a new type of assessment and were part of a conscious attempt to move away from traditional standardized written test procedures. The TGAT approach was one which emphasized a wide range of types of assessment *task* rather than just tests, involving different types of response – oral, written, practical – in order to reduce the negative and narrowing impact on curriculum coverage traditionally associated with formal external high-stakes assessment through teaching to the test. For example, HMI (1979) reported the stultifying effect of the O-level exam on the curriculum in secondary schools. Similarly, in the days of the 11+ primary school work was devoted largely to the basic skills and verbal reasoning type of tasks which featured in the exam; when the 11+ was phased out the curriculum in primary schools broadened (Gipps 1988b).

The style of assessment in SATs was essentially active and based on good infant school practice, and teachers in 1991 (and 1992) had some choice of SATs in maths and science. Multiplication, subtraction and addition were assessed through children throwing dice, as in a game, and having to add or multiply the numbers thrown; they were asked to design their own dice game to assess the process targets in mathematics. Floating and sinking, in science, were approached through a practical task in which the children were provided with a range of objects and a large tank of water. Assessment of reading at the level expected for seven-year-olds took the form of children reading aloud from a book chosen from a range of appropriate storybooks: children were assessed for fluency as they read, and then asked questions when they had finished in order to test their comprehension. There were also traditional 'paper and pencil' tasks to be done in maths on illustrated worksheets. The children had to write a story in which their handwriting, spelling and creative writing were assessed. On the whole, though, the children did not have to write their answers: in science, for example, teachers were allowed to help children produce written answers and were allowed to make their own judgments about whether the child understood or was able to do the task in hand, regardless of whether the child had been able to write it down. Children whose mother tongue was not English were allowed to have an interpreter for the maths and science tasks; as we shall see, this, despite best intentions, was a process fraught with difficulties as far as the assessment was concerned.

Another area where SATs differed from traditional standardized tests was in the instructions given to the teacher and to the child; in SATs the most important consideration was that children should understand what was expected of them, thus there was no restriction on what was said to the child, provided, of course, that the teacher did not give the answer to the question. There was no restriction on non-linguistic methods of presentation, no restriction on the use of another adult who was normally present in the classroom and no restriction on pupils working in whatever language they wished, or normally used, in the maths or science tasks. However, pupils were not allowed to explain the tasks to each other, and those whose mother tongue was not English could not have the help of an interpreter for the English SATs.

The 1991 experience

For Y2 teachers the first national implementation of SATs was a traumatic experience. For the average Y2 class of 25–30 children, doing the SATs took between 40 and 45 hours of direct teacher time. In some schools the time taken to do the individual reading assessments was in addition to this (NFER/BGC 1992). The fact that only small groups could do the SATs at any one time raised questions of classroom and time management. Many teachers reported that, before the tests took place, they had spent considerable time over the Easter holiday preparing themselves and the test materials.

On our first visit to schools we had specifically noted and asked about the layout of the classrooms, the type of activities planned, use of staff in the class, the teacher's preferred mode of operating with children and how the children were grouped.

SATs as a 'built-in' activity

When we observed the SATs on our second visit to the 32 project schools, teachers in 12 of the classrooms were operating in a very similar way to that observed on our first visit. As one headteacher put it: 'Teachers are absorbing SATs into normal practice.' These 12 teachers were operating 'normally' in that:

- the use of space and seating was exactly or very nearly the same as on the first visit;
- the whole class had been planned for by the class teacher, with the SAT group just one of many;
- the activities were similar to those observed previously;
- non-SAT children did activities similar to the SATs;
- timetabled activities were not necessarily disrupted by SATs;
- the staff in classrooms were deployed (that is, the classroom was managed) in the same way as on our first visit.

Eight of these 12 teachers had ancillary help present in the classroom but maintained total control of classroom management and curriculum content: they did all the re-routeing, dealt with issues of discipline, answered children's questions, stopped the SAT group when they wanted, or left the SAT group alone and circulated around the others, as they normally did. The ancillaries supervised other activities or heard reading as usual. These teachers were, therefore, observed to be operating in a way closely resembling that of visit one: dealing with whole-class issues, sometimes addressing the whole class, going round all groups or working with one group at a time, but occasionally circulating and always controlling the activities of the whole class.

It could be said, then, that in 12 classrooms, SATs were 'built in' to the usual working pattern. However, three teachers in this group maintained their usual management processes by adopting ritual. This consisted of pinning on badges or bows as a sign that they should not be disturbed. The badges and bows symbolised that the teachers were 'off-limits' assessing the SAT group and must not be approached. Once this separation of the SAT group was achieved the teachers were freed from interruption. On one occasion, it was difficult to keep the SAT group apart: the non-SAT children forgot the rules. In this case, when a non-SAT child approached the teacher, the teacher merely pointed to her badge, no words were exchanged and the child moved off.

SATs as 'bolt-on' activity

In the other 20 schools the way in which SATs were managed led to a certain 'artificiality' in daily classroom routine. One headteacher called it 'a false situation, totally controlled and unreal in the classroom'. Twelve of these classrooms had been reorganized to provide a special SAT area – usually two tables and five chairs (one for each child and the teacher) – in a corner or other part of the classroom that was somehow separate. The other children usually seemed to know that this area was meant only for SAT activities.

Teachers and heads in these 20 schools gave three reasons for this sense of artificiality:

- planning two separate timetables / different activities (i.e. for the SAT group and the rest of the class)
- intensive concentration on the SAT groups
- giving away responsibility for the rest of the class.

One teacher with a vertically grouped class thought she would be able to work SATs into her usual 'class structure', but could not. Instead, she planned in an artificial way during the SATs period: one timetable for Y2 and another for Y3. Normally, she would plan for the class as a whole regardless of year group. Another teacher mentioned that Y2 children were getting less timetabled PE because that time was being used for SATS, and a third was observed to withdraw children from assembly.

One headteacher mentioned how the teachers were more tired because of 'intensive concentration' on small numbers of children. Withdrawing children from the classroom, as a strategy for implementation, may have exacerbated this. Seventeen schools in this group of 20 withdrew children: five for reading only; eight for other SATs only; and four for both reading and other SATs. The other three teachers did not leave the classroom but neither did they leave the SAT group during the assessment. The fact that they did not leave the SAT group could have led to a feeling of intensive concentration and also to an unfamiliar feeling of being 'unavailable' to non-SAT children, which was mentioned by two of these teachers.

To support SATs in these schools, other adults were introduced into classrooms. These other adults were headteachers, English as a second language (E2L) teachers, supply teachers, support teachers, special needs teachers, and ancillary staff such as nursery assistants, parents, students and colleagues. Teachers either gave small groups into the care of others or gave responsibility for the rest of the class to someone else, while they themselves took a small group. In ten schools teachers seemed willingly to accept the help of others and made no reference to this extra help being artificial to classroom processes. However, the other ten teachers made special mention of the support, saying that it added to the artificiality that SATs lent to daily routine. From comments made in their interviews, and from our observation, it was noted that these ten teachers accommodated help but were ambivalent about it.

For teachers in these 20 schools, then, SATs meant all or most of the following changes:

- newly created classroom layouts and withdrawal groups;
- planning different activities for year groups;
- sharing teaching and giving away responsibility;
- operating in a different way (e.g. being unavailable to some children).

What emerges, however, is that, regardless of whether the SATs were integrated into the normal teaching activity or bolted on to it, considerable extra effort and organization were involved for the teacher.

The 1992 experience

There was widespread publicity at the time of the 1991 tests, with articles in the newspapers about the amount of time that the Y2 SATs were taking; the Prime Minister, therefore, announced in the summer of 1991 (before any formal evaluations of the SATs were available), that the tests for 1992 would be shorter, more standardized, paper and pencil tests. The 1992 SATs, as a result, contained fewer active assessment tasks, but were by no means all paper and pencil tests. For a number of SATs a whole-class administrative procedure was offered but, in fact, few teachers in our study took up this option, feeling that testing six- and seven-year-olds in a whole-class context was not appropriate. The reading SAT continued to be a reading-aloud task, with the teacher making a running record of children's errors and an accuracy score. Two extra tests were introduced: a traditional reading comprehension test with a written response, and a standardized spelling test. Both of these were in traditional booklet form, to be administered in large groups with no teacher involvement, with the reading test being optional for children who scored at level 2 and above, while the spelling test was compulsory for those who scored at level 3 and above in English and spelling. For the first time the results from the reading and spelling tests had to be reported separately alongside the score for the maths 'number' attainment target as well as the overall levels for English, maths and science.

The testing in 1992 took on average 24 hours of class time for a class of 25–30 children; in addition to this, there was the time for individual reading assessments (NFER/BGC 1992). This was a considerable reduction from the 40–45 hours in 1991. Second time around, the testing was managed with less stress, partly because schools knew what to expect, partly because two long practical tasks (one in maths and one in science) were dropped. However, the testing still took a considerable amount of time and arrangements still had to made for other children while individuals or small groups were tested. We found, again, that the administration was by no means standardized, so that both reliability and manageability were still major issues.

For the testing in 1992 the Curriculum Orders in maths and science were also modified. While generally welcoming the simplification of the curriculum and its structure and the reduction in the number of ATs to be assessed, the general feeling was that since there were more statements of attainment under each new AT it would be more difficult for children to get a level. Only two of the 31 headteachers felt that the new AT structures were better than the old ones. In relation to the slimmed-down SATs for 1992, the headteachers welcomed the reduction in time that would be involved, but were generally anxious about the introduction of more paper and pencil testing which would lead, they felt, to a regression to formal work at primary school level. A few of the headteachers, three out of 31, regretted the demise of SATs covering the process ATs since the children had enjoyed them and their presence had made the process parts of the curriculum important; other head-teachers were pleased to see those tasks go because of the time involved. There was a general anxiety that if the tests were more formal some of the children would be more anxious than in 1991, when the children tended not to see the SATs as being particularly different from classwork (Pollard *et al.* 1994). In anticipation, there was a general feeling that the new slimmed-down SATs, if they were more paper and pencil than small-group orientated, would be harder for the children and cause more anxiety.

In 1992 we observed the SATs in 18 schools and interviewed in the remaining five schools where we could not observe. In the eight other schools left in the project, the Y2 teacher had changed. It was decided to focus only on the 23 schools in which the Y2 teacher remained the same so as to obtain an indication of change between 1991 and 1992. We observed the full range of SATs and were sometimes able to watch a whole Y2 class complete SATs in one subject. We also observed the same SAT in a number of schools. Our emphasis here was on consistency and comparability across teachers and administrations. It seemed as though manageability was not going to be a particular issue this time around.

In the event, time was still a significant issue, although most teachers felt that the SATs were quicker and easier to do in 1992. Despite the provision for whole-class testing, only a small minority of teachers attempted this, and usually only with story-writing. Indeed, some teachers felt that the 1992 tasks were *less* suited to group testing than those in 1991, mainly because of the possibility of children copying or listening in. Consequently, some teachers conducted SATs with individual children to an even greater extent than they had the previous year, especially in science. The maths tasks were also thought to require small groups so that the teacher could watch for copying and help children keep their places on the complicated answer sheets.

Most schools withdrew children for reading, as in 1991. SATs in groups were usually done in the classroom, although sometimes groups were withdrawn to other areas, or the rest of the class was withdrawn.

Value of the tasks

Most teachers felt that 1992's SATs reflected good teaching practice, 'the kind of thing we would be doing anyway', and some planned to use the SATs for their TA the following year: one school put the SATs in its 'bank' of work to be used for TA throughout the school.

While some teachers welcomed the quicker, easier maths and science SATs, a few bemoaned the loss of the previous year's maths game and the floating and sinking work in science; 'those were really a test of thinking processes'. On the other hand, the faster completion of SATs was very important to most teachers and one felt that the loss of the previous year's maths game was 'the best thing about this year's SATs'.

Teachers liked some of the tasks and some of the changes introduced in 1992. The most popular change seemed to be the introduction of letter grades to grade performance more finely within reading level 2. Teachers commented very positively on the usefulness and accuracy of these grades; no one commented negatively. Some wished that the letter grades could also be used at level 1. The reading assessment was generally liked by the teachers and there were no complaints at all about the reading SAT itself; one teacher (a systematic assessor) described the reading running record as a 'good diagnostic tool'. There were, however, many negative feelings towards the reading comprehension test 'At the Funfair'. About half the teachers chose to do the comprehension test, mostly because they believed they 'had' to do it, or it was 'strongly recommended' by either the headteacher or the LEA. A few did it out of curiosity. At least one LEA (Midboro) apparently advised teachers *not* to do it and in some cases it arrived too late to do at the specified time.

Three teachers did not do it because the materials were 'bad' or 'too difficult'; it was generally felt that the test was 'middle-class' and 'too difficult for our children'.

Mental arithmetic was still tested in an activity where children had to give answers to simple mental problems within a five-second time limit, and this SAT brought the most negative comment: some teachers found the five-second time limit caused 'panic' in children, while others felt that the time limit was irrelevant anyway if the child could do the sums. At least three teachers were seen to ignore the five-second time limit altogether. Interestingly, two teachers felt that five seconds was too long, allowing enough time for children to count on their fingers. Generally though, teachers felt that some children felt under pressure by the time limit. This SAT, as it turned out, following a similar task in the previous year, was to have a major impact on teachers' practice.

Differentiation

In both 1991 and 1992 children could be entered for the SAT at either level 1 or level 2 depending on the teacher's estimate of their attainment. Some teachers made this entry decision in relation to their formal TA but more often based on their general knowledge of working with the children – 'just gauging what you know about them'. If children failed on the level at which they were entered, teachers were supposed to give them the task one level below. However, not all our teachers did that; in particular, if they felt that the children would easily succeed on the easier task then they did not bother to waste time giving it to them. Similarly, where pupils succeeded on a particular level teachers were required to enter them for the next higher level. However, again, teachers did not always do this if they felt concerned that children would not succeed.

In 1992, for the first time, seven-year-olds were given the opportunity to take SATs at level 4, one level higher than in 1991 and the level at which an average 11-year-old would be expected to perform. We asked teachers specifically about whether they had taken children up to the higher levels. It was clear that some teachers saw level 3 as going quite high enough and in some cases teachers within a school had an agreed policy – 'level 3 is good enough for us'. In other schools, teachers had different views and one teacher might be entering her children for level 4, with another teacher in the same school not doing so; this, of course, has implications for the comparability of results across schools.

The four LEAs themselves transmitted different degrees of enthusiasm to their teachers about the appropriateness of level 4. One LEA reminded teachers that the children were entitled to try level 4, so if they passed at level 3 they should all be given the opportunity to try level 4. Another LEA was more cautious and advised teachers to seek a second opinion from advisory teachers about whether it was appropriate to give a particular child a level 4 task. In the third LEA, heads were asked to implement the level 4 SATs themselves, or to check the teachers' judgements. In the fourth LEA it was implied that achievement of level 4 would be very rare indeed. The different approach from LEAs needs to be seen, we feel, not in the light of a negative attitude towards raising children's attainment, but as a result of a genuine lack of experience with, and understanding of, the pitching of the levels within the national curriculum. It should be remembered that the entire level-based national curriculum had only been in operation for three years by this time, and teachers had no experience of level 4 work or even much of level 3 work for seven-year-olds. That said, however, the differing policy advice to schools can be seen to have a direct influence on the reliability of the results. On the other hand, it was clear that the teachers in our schools treated the LEA advice in a cavalier fashion, and schools and teachers made up their own minds about whether to offer level 4.

Some of the 18 teachers who did use the level 4 SATs did so to fulfil the letter of the law – 'I would try them to say I'd done them'. Others did so 'just for interest' or to 'let them have a go', to get a real idea of the child's ability.

> If a child can do level 3, it's reasonable to go on so you as a teacher can see where a child actually is.

Of the 13 teachers who did not offer level 4 SATs, some had planned in advance to go no further than level 3; one of these teachers had no level 3 children in any case. Of particular interest to us was why these teachers did not give the children advanced tasks. The reasons given can be divided into four categories. The first category was teachers' own preconceived expectations for children:

> There is no way the children would achieve all of it; bits perhaps but not all.

They are not conceptually ready for the science.

Children would have to be brilliant or gifted.

No one's got a hope of level 4.

The second was bound up with views of the differences between infant children and junior children and the curriculum appropriate for each:

Six-year-olds are not mature enough.

The materials are Key Stage 2 work which has not been planned into teaching.

They are good materials for junior colleagues to look at.

The third addressed the implications for the curriculum in Years 3–6 if children were attaining level 4 in Year 2:

Where would you go next?

Finally, there was general criticism of the national assessment criteria and levels:

Seven-year-olds can't be like 11-year-olds.

After SATs, two headteachers felt embarrassment and disbelief at finding level 4s:

I hadn't intended to achieve so many level 4s.

We had one here and it was a bit embarrassing. I had to call in the moderator.

For some teachers, then, concern over assessments at level 4 caused them to question the underlying structure of the national curriculum. Although it was always planned that the national curriculum levels would be reviewed to see whether they were pitched appropriately, as far as schools and teachers were concerned they were as given, and indeed had to be worked with as they stood.

The 1993 experience

For 1993 there were further changes to the SATs, with the name changed to Standard Tasks and Standard Tests (we continue to refer to them as 'SATs', as teachers still do), and a further reduction of process activities. The spelling and reading comprehension tests were made compulsory for all children except at level 1, the maths and science tests focused on algebra, as well as number, and physics, the idea being that apart from the number AT which would always be assessed, a different AT in maths and science would be assessed each year in a rolling programme. The testing package was to take around 30 hours of classroom time, much as it did in 1992, this being achieved again by the science and maths tasks being essentially worksheet-based rather than active. Thus, by 1993, at Key Stage 1 there was a mixture of standard tasks (performance-type assessments) and more traditional standardized tests.

In the event, the teachers' unions called for a boycott of national assessment in 1993. As a result of the boycott, the government set up a committee under the chairmanship of Sir Ron Dearing to review the entire national curriculum and assessment programme with the express aim that ways be found to simplify the testing programme.

Before the NAPS project ended, we had received funding from the ESRC to extend our research into assessment at Key Stage 2. We asked our original schools if they wanted to continue working with us and eight infant (or first) schools and 11 primary schools agreed to carry on. It was from the headteachers of these 19 schools and the four assessment advisers that we collected data on SATs in 1993. What had happened? Had the teachers completed everything? How had the action of the unions affected things? What did headteachers think of results, and who else had access to them?

Union action

In 1992 and early 1993, there had been much debate among the teachers' unions and professional associations as to whether teachers should boycott the SATs, and one adviser felt that assessment in particular had been targeted as 'a symbolic way of rebelling against central control'. In March 1993, the NAS/UWT declared a boycott on all national curriculum assessment because of the perceived extra workload (approximately 116 hours) to mark the Key Stage 3 tests. Indeed, it was the English teachers at Key Stage 3 who were particularly vocal in their arguments. Another adviser explained how 'the whole boycott issue arose out of KS3' and implied that if it hadn't been for the Key Stage 3 outcry, Key Stage 1 teachers would probably have carried on quietly with SATs and taken no action:

> the teachers at Key Stage 1 were part-way through their formal assessments then suddenly – whoosh – they were faced with the union boycott and it became very high-profile publicly.

The General Secretary of the National Union of Teachers (NUT), Douglas McAvoy, declared that the tests themselves were unsound and that they told teachers nothing new – it was time the government stopped punishing teachers and pupils (*Channel 4 News*, 7 April 1993) Consequently, in mid-May teachers in the NUT received an explicit directive and union advice was spelled out:

- Reception teachers should continue to teach but not cover for SATs;
- Y1 teachers should restructure the amount of TA they were doing and do no SATs work;
- Y2 teachers should not start SATs. If they were half-way through, they were to stop. If they were nearly finished, they were to stop;
- All work on moderation and aggregation was to cease.

(Homeshire adviser)

In all four LEAs the headteachers were caught between the devil and the deep blue sea. The union to which many of them belonged, the National Association of Head Teachers (NAHT), had advised them to keep out of the dispute, but they had a legal obligation to report to parents and if the boycott went ahead they would have only sketchy data or no numbers at all to hand. Consequently, there was a flurry of phone calls to the advisers for support and for information on what everyone else was doing. In the end, headteachers were to come to some agreement with their teachers as to what to present to parents, because, at heart, most felt strongly that 'the professional aspect of reporting to parents was worth doing' (Midboro LEA).

The boycott made it more difficult for the LEA advisers to do their job. The assessment adviser in Midboro reported that:

> the union action makes it difficult to talk to people formally about assessment when they aren't supposed to be doing it.

In Homeshire they explained how 'the boycott had caused chaos for planning any training'. Some schools were 'dropping everything to do with the national curriculum and national assessment' and this meant dropping out of training for Key Stage 2. Because schools were unlikely to report results, any analysis of Key Stage 1 results at LEA level was out of the question. When we asked the heads whether their Y2 teachers had completed the SATs, only one replied that they had not even started, and this was because there was no one on the staff who could have administered them (the two Y2 teachers were absent). Her union had supported her decision although the LEA had not. Seven heads explained that the teachers had worked 'until the vote was announced and then stopped'. One of these heads reported that although most of his teachers were in the NUT:

> they were very professional in the way they approached it; they didn't, like some people, anticipate the boycott and not start at all.

Another headteacher was pleased that they had completed everything except the reading comprehension before they stopped, because 'we didn't want to kowtow to anybody, we thought it was a good exercise to do'. (The Homeshire adviser felt that 'even the most moderate teachers had refused to do the spelling and comprehension as a contribution to the union action'.) In contrast, a third headteacher admitted feeling a sense of relief when everything stopped because the staff had been extremely 'rankled' by the boycott. They had been provoked by the outcry of the Key Stage 3 teachers into thinking 'Why didn't *we* do that?' and wished they had been more militant.

Eleven heads reported that their Y2 teachers had gone ahead and completed all the statutory tasks. (Some had even done the voluntary SATs in history and geography.) Headteachers felt that they did not want to disadvantage the children, waste all that time spent on teachers' TA and preparation or (in one or two cases) break a chain of results they had amassed and used for school review over the previous three years. The general feeling was that union advice came too late:

> Key Stage 1 teachers have come to the end of a long hard process and don't see the point of the action now.
>
> (Homeshire LEA)

I've started so I'll finish.

(Northshire headteacher)

Testing under the boycott

We had not planned to do much fieldwork in schools in that summer, fortuitously as it turned out. On approaching our schools later in the summer, however, we found that many had indeed done the SATs, although they would not report the results to the LEA. We, therefore, did interview 11 Y2 teachers who remained from our original sample and who had done the SATs three years running. This year our teachers were more critical of the tasks, which was no doubt a reflection of their experience with SATs over the years, but also, we felt, to do with the quality of the worksheets. Almost half of the teachers (in general, the systematic planners) disapproved of the paper and pencil approach with the worksheets. They criticized the tasks as too shallow – they 'have no substance, are bitty', 'just a tick and they're finished', 'mostly secondhand experience' – and the general feeling from these teachers was that the tests were narrower and not particularly good. This seems to stem from the fact that this sort of task, essentially worksheet-based rather than interactive, was not in line with their way of teaching.

One teacher suggested that the children also found the tasks alien to their usual ways of working:

> They can't believe the simplicity of some of the tasks and get creative with their answers.

They were not used to paper and pencil tests: when one boy was ready to start a science task he left his seat to go and find the magnets. When the teacher told him this was not allowed, he was indignant: 'But you said that science was about experimenting with things.' It made the teacher think:

> When have I ever done any science without using equipment? It's a paper and pencil test with no substance. You wouldn't normally work like this.

Higher levels

In 1993 children could again be assessed at level 4. Four teachers had made the decision to stop at level 3. In one case this was because, although the teacher had had level 4 children in 1992, there was no moderator available in 1993 and the teacher did not feel confident enough to assess at level 4 without the moderator's support. Two had made a decision to stop at level 3:

> we don't foresee any level 3s. We don't have any level 4 children here.

Another four teachers were taking children on to higher levels but felt pressurized into it and were not always in favour. For one headteacher the pressure was coming from the government and the media, the implication being that if schools did not get any level 4 children, teachers were underestimating them. There was still a feeling among headteachers that, as a rule, children aged 7 should not be getting level 4. In the case of infant schools, there was anxiety about sending level 4 and indeed level 3 children up to the junior school:

> the junior school will wonder how that child got that when he doesn't know it now.

Preparation for SATs

It became clear from these interviews, however, that teachers were now preparing the children for SATs in very specific ways, for example, doing grammar and sentence worksheets and preparing them for particular tasks in science. Teachers in four of these schools were adapting the SATs or the worksheets if they thought them unsuitable or confusing, and using drawing and talking as well as written responses.

Although we did not ask the teachers directly if they felt they were teaching to the test, it seems that only two schools had made no effort whatsoever to prepare the children for the SATs in 1993. In the other nine schools where we worked there was clear evidence of preparing directly for the 1993 SATS. Eight of the teachers were preparing specifically for the science task which was now considered to require specific content knowledge. The input varied from teaching the words so that they could read the test paper to doing a quick input on the topics before the SAT, giving practice on worksheets similar to the SATs, and working on the topic covered in the SAT in the period preceding the SAT term. Two examples from one of the LEAs are interesting: the advice from this LEA was that the science test on AT4 was knowledge-based. The advisory teacher apparently advised the teachers to teach this content three weeks, or one week, before the SAT but not the day before. One of the schools did not accept this advice, believing that science 'was supposed to be about processes' and did not need specific preparation. Nevertheless, the school did do projects on these topics in time for the SAT. Another teacher had a glimpse of the SATs immediately after Christmas and 'wanted the children to get some experience with magnets and electricity'. This teacher was adamant that:

> of course, we would not consider teaching to the test, but we had to make sure it was fair to all the children, so we made the equipment available. We worked on 'repelling' a bit because they didn't understand.

In maths, teachers would prepare workcards that laid out the sums in the same way that they were on the SAT worksheets. They let the children practise reading aloud with accuracy and expression, as they were required to do in the reading SAT. In one school children were given handwriting patterns to practise at home so that some could achieve level 3 in handwriting.

For the most part teachers gave this account of preparing the children for the test materials in a rather embarrassed way. As far as the heads were concerned, however, the view was more pragmatic: preparing the children for the test was inevitable as they had to be seen to be getting good results.

Overall, the teachers that we revisited in 1993 were divided between getting the SATs over and done with and leaving them as late as possible in the summer term so that children had a chance to cover the work. These teachers were generally unhappy about the 1993 SATs: they criticized the paper and pencil approach and identified many difficulties and unsuitable features in the individual pupil worksheets. Schools varied in their attitudes towards taking children up to the higher levels but there was still a resistance to doing level 4 and the attitude of the receiving school was now brought into the equation. These teachers had geared up for the SATs in 1993 and there was clear evidence of preparing the children for the SATs in all three core areas.

The 1994 experience

In 1994 there was a second boycott by the NUT only, which was still not satisfied either with the quality of the tests or with the valuing of external tests over TA. Nevertheless, in July 1994 we sent out a questionnaire to 28 Y2 teachers in schools working with us on the second phase (NAPS 2, ESRC reference no. R000 23 4438). Seventeen questionnaires were returned, revealing five schools as having boycotted the SATs, while 12 had done them. Four teachers had also done the non-statutory SATs in history, geography and technology; these teachers had found them useful to back up their TA.

In the 12 schools where SATs had been done, only one child had been excluded ('not capable; only on level W–1'). As our schools ranged from small infant to large primary, the numbers of children tested ranged from 12 to 47. Schools varied in the amount of time taken over SATs: the least time was reported by one school as eight and a half days, while three schools spread it over a month, four over half a term and four over a whole term.

In 1994 science was dropped from statutory assessment, leaving only maths and English to be assessed by SATs. Thus in 1994 Y2 teachers assessed science by TA only, and they did this in different ways. Four teachers used the optional SAT materials from 1993 and 1994 to assess science in an ongoing way throughout the year. Three teachers used a combination of their own methods ('simple practical tasks', 'assessment sheets at the end of topics') and some of the SAT materials. Five did not use the SAT materials but used their own methods in a continuous fashion (observation, written responses, questions, discussion, and children's own recording).

Six teachers made no changes to their usual forms of organization to accommodate SATs, while the other six did. The changes involved new ways of grouping children, withdrawing children from assembly, 'removing or isolating children not being tested' and spending a lot of time on assessment activities instead of teaching. When asked if SATs had been easy to fit in (even if changes had been made) two teachers did not appreciate having to rearrange groups, and one did not like to concentrate for longer than usual on one group:

> I don't usually spend three quarters of an hour with one group of children, with no contact with the rest of the class.

However, the other nine did not mind making the changes because they found SATs easy to fit in. Of these teachers three said they were easy to fit in because of the way they had organized it (that is, by the way they had used the support available or by the way they had worked with colleagues or by doing SATs with the whole class).

Comparing assessments

We asked teachers in 1994 how they felt the SAT results compared with TA. One teacher made no comment on results at all, one said they used SATs for TA (and therefore the question was presumably redundant), while nine teachers said that the SAT results were 'very similar to', 'close to' or 'more or less the same' as their TAs. The other teacher commented specifically on her maths results, saying that in 22 out of 28 cases SATs and TA tallied 'but in three cases the children performed better and in three cases . . . worse' than on TA; she had explanations for the three who had fallen below her expectations – 'one child was not well, two were anxious' – but not for those who had exceeded them.

When we asked the teachers how the results compared with those of previous years, four said they did not know, but eight gave answers: three said the results were 'similar' to or the 'same' as last year's; one mused, 'it seems to be the norm for our school – I don't know why', and two said the results were slightly better. One said that the reason for this was 'smaller classes' and another said it was because she had changed the curriculum:

> slight change to the English work done prior to SATs – more emphasis on sentence construction.

The other three said that results were lower in some way. One teacher mentioned that maths results were down because 'we had not covered formal multiplication'. The other two said results were poorer because the children were 'less capable' than last year's group.

Part of our questionnaire was specifically aimed at teachers who had done SATs before, whether or not they had completed them in 1994. In these teachers we had a full range of experience: three had taught Y2 since the start of national assessment and had carried out SATs four times; three had done them three times; five had done them twice; and one once. Three teachers could not tell us whether the 1994 SATs were easier to carry out because they had boycotted in 1993 and could not make comparisons. However, the other nine had something to report. Only one teacher (who had done SATs three times before) said they were not easier because 'there was no significant reduction in workload'. The other eight said they were easier because they were 'simple', 'easy to administer', 'there were less of them', they could be done in larger groups and the guidelines were clear. Two of these teachers reported increased confidence, having done SATs twice before, and another said they were easier 'because of the way we organized them'.

Twelve teachers had something to say about changes in SATs over time. One Innercity teacher, who had done SATs twice before, despised tests at Key Stage 1 on principle and felt that any changes had not been for the better:

> We do not agree with the principle of testing at seven years old.
> Tests are still inappropriate, particularly for bilingual pupils.

Among the other 11 teachers, however, there was a feeling that certain aspects of the SATs had improved. On the issue of content, two felt that they were better. On the issue of manageability, six felt that they were generally easy to administer; one said that the marking guidelines had improved while one said there was less pressure. In an interview with one of our NAPS 1 teachers, who had worked with us for four years, she said:

> We just felt that if you blink you'll miss it this year.

Are SATs worth doing?

The experienced Y2 teachers who carried out the SATs in 1994 were equally divided as to what they thought. Six of the 12 thought that SATs were not worth doing, five of them because 'ongoing teacher assessment would be adequate'. Other reasons given were: 'it takes up valuable teaching time' and 'I neglect my Y1 children during the weeks I administer them'.

Six teachers thought SATs *were* worth doing, four because they moderated or confirmed TA and ensured teachers were working to the same standards, and two because the materials themselves were useful 'for ideas on how to test and assess'. One of these teachers also acknowledged that 'the time spent with individual children is excellent'.

Another question was whether SATs are fair to all children. Thirteen teachers had an opinion on this (one who boycotted SATs gave an opinion). Four thought SATs *were* fair to all because teachers had entered children at appropriate levels in the first place, they were standardized throughout England and Wales, and TA could always override the SAT result, through the moderator, if need be. Nine thought SATs *were not* fair to all children. Four reasons were given for this. First, children were of different ages when they sat the tests and there was no weighting given for this. Second, SATs as tests were not appropriate for some seven-year-olds: 'Some can't read them and feel threatened', 'exam conditions are not appropriate for some children', 'they put pressure on children' and 'E2L children must be at a disadvantage'. Third, they 'do not illustrate an individual's achievement and progress'. Fourth, 'they are open to being misused'.

The SAT as an 'objective' assessment

In assessment parlance an objective test is one which does not rely on qualitative judgements of performance; the classic objective test is the multiple-choice test in which the individual taking the test ticks one of the set of prespecified answers. These tests can be machine-marked, thus removing any problem of variability across markers. Standardized tests, which may not be multiple-choice tests but invite a written response, are given in standardized or controlled conditions, with all individuals receiving the same instructions and with testing conditions as similar as possible for all. In both cases this is done in order to enhance comparability of results, through a consistent approach.

The SATs were neither 'objective' nor standardized: teachers were given considerable scope to explain the tasks to children, with the instruction that they should do what was necessary to make sure that the children understood the task. Although this approach was well intended, it caused problems in the consistent presentation of tasks to pupils. The lack of standardized introduction for the assessment tasks meant that, as we and other researchers (Gipps *et al.* 1992; James and Conner, 1993; Abbott *et al.* 1994; Pollard *et al.* 1994) observed, there was considerable variation in the administration of the SATs, not only from one teacher to another but also when SATs were given to different children by the same teacher. This was to some extent intended since some variation in presentation was considered to be more appropriate and fair at this age than highly standardized procedures. The TGAT was not concerned with 'objectivity', more with fairness and validity, allowing variability in presentation to give children the maximum chance to perform well. It should be remembered, of course, that this was in the context of the TGAT's recommendation that results at age 7 should not be published. Unfortunately, the government became more and more concerned with objectivity, failing to appreciate that in the process of achieving this we may be reducing validity.

Allowing variability makes comparability harder to control, and we observed that some presentations were easier than others, for example, where the teacher gave fuller instructions to one child than another, or one set of objects to sort was easier to group and categorize than another.

Our observations of SATs in 1994 indicate that there was still variability across teachers in how they organized and presented SATs; even the more formal and standardized reading comprehension test 'Toys and Games' varied in the way it was organized and presented, which we felt was affecting the difficulty of the task and children's ability to perform at their best. After a short practice test, the children had to read a glossy booklet of four stories and give their answers in a separate paper booklet. Some of the answers were multiple-choice and only required a tick, while others asked the children to write out a phrase or sentence. The comfort, space and quietness of the conditions for testing varied, as did the amount of time spent on the testing, which ranged from one hour to two and a quarter hours. Apart from these timing issues, other elements that varied were the teacher's state, her relationships and interaction with the children, her general testing 'mode' and interruptions.

In an assessment programme where results were to be used only within the school by the class teacher this variability and hence difficulty across administration of the SATs would have little consequence. However, in a national assessment programme where the results are intended to be used for reporting and accountability purposes any variation in difficulty across teachers, across schools, and across children within the same classroom threatens comparability and is patently unfair. The prime requirement of any assessment programme that is used for monitoring or accountability purposes is that the assessment across schools and individuals be consistent so that the results are comparable. These SATs, however, were a new form of assessment and these problems and difficulties were not foreseen.

To conclude, the SATs as external tests were part of the national assessment programme in order to ensure that there was an 'objective' aspect to the assessment programme. Assessments made by teachers are essentially 'subjective', so the argument goes, and tests external to the teacher devised outside the school offer a more 'objective' and, therefore, reliable assessment of pupils. Although the SAT tasks were indeed designed outside the school, there was a considerable element of teacher judgement and teacher control in the SAT administration and marking, and the tests did not, therefore, subscribe to the idea of a truly external 'objective test' as anticipated by central government. In the final chapter we comment, however, on the effect of doing these SATs on teachers' assessment skills.

4

MANAGING CHANGE WITHIN SCHOOLS

Schools were, in the main, totally unprepared for the impact of the national curriculum and its assessment programme in 1991. Not only did Y1 and Y2 teachers have to teach a new and specified curriculum in the core subjects, English, maths and science (which for many infant teachers meant taking on science for the first time), but also Y2 teachers had to make their own assessment across the ATs (involving 228 statements of attainment as assessment criteria) and administer the SATs to all their Y2 pupils. The workload which all this entailed was not, and could not have been, fully appreciated. The training available to schools and the variable nature of it is outlined in the next chapter. We now look at the way in which heads approached this multiple innovation and helped their teachers through it, and in a later section we look at how teachers reacted to the changes.

Heads' management for SATs

In 1991, heads, not surprisingly, varied in the amount and type of changes which they made to support their teachers. Some were low-key, having made very few changes to accommodate SATs. At the other extreme were the schools which reported total disruption, involving shunting staff, retimetabling the school day, cancelling meetings and activities and reallocating space and resources. In one school virtually nothing remained unchanged:

> The reception/Y1 teacher leaves her own class to do all the reading SATs on three mornings per week, while the nursery teacher takes the reception class and two nursery nurses look after the nursery. Any parents who want to help are put in reception; the reception's full time auxiliary is put into one Y2 class while another auxiliary, who normally works with a child with recognized special educational needs, is moved to the other Y2 class. Classes are doubled up for story time and assembly has been changed from mid-morning to first thing. INSET attendance and curriculum development meetings are stopped and teachers, other than Y2, take on more assembly and playground duties. The head, as a moderator, is out of school for up to 22 days with no supply cover available.
>
> (Field notes)

Five headteachers were moderators for the LEA. This in itself was sometimes seen as support because information and advice were readily available to be filtered down to the Y2 teacher. On the other hand, headteachers who were moderators were out of their own schools much of the time and may have been unavailable to offer active support in the same way as non-moderating headteachers.

In half of the 32 schools, heads themselves took an active role; six took classes while teachers administered SATs in another room; five carried out some or all of the reading SATs themselves, usually at level 3, which is the most time-consuming; one was observed doing a science SAT. Other headteachers helped out in classrooms for a set period each week, or contributed support by taking more assemblies or dealing with equipment. In the 16 schools where headteachers did not get actively involved (for example, because of moderation or teaching duties), support from other quarters was usually provided. In most of these schools teachers worked in informal teams of three or four and were assumed to support each other. In fact, they did: in five of the schools, with some form of team-teaching, Y2 teachers reported 'good collegial support' and seemed to derive mutual support and satisfaction from working together. In three schools Y2 teachers, who did not normally work in teams, had refused help from their colleagues, although the nature of this help was not clear. The seven teachers who were the only Y2 teachers in their schools often received sympathy rather than practical help from their colleagues.

High- and low-support schools

It became clear to us that schools varied enormously in terms of the amount of support put in for the SAT experience. We derived a classification to identify schools at the extremes of high and low support so that we could look at what made a school offer high or low levels of help, and what effect this had.

High-support schools were defined as those in which all of the following support was made available to Y2 teachers:

- heads actively involved in SATs either by taking the rest of the class, by doing a SAT themselves or by helping out in the classroom;
- supply or support teaching staff (in addition to those normally used) available for all or part of the SATs period;
- other kinds of support made available, such as ancillaries, non-contact time, excusal from playground duties or assemblies, and availability of other rooms and resources.

Five high-support schools were identified by these criteria. In four, some SATs were carried out by someone other than the Y2 teacher; in two cases, reading was done by someone else; in four cases science was done by someone else; in two cases all or part of the maths SATs were done by someone else. The high-support schools generally had heads who were anxious to protect teachers, especially teachers who were seen to be vulnerable. In one school the Y2 teacher was also deputy head (becoming acting head the following September), assessment co-ordinator and a moderator and, therefore, out of her own classroom for 18 days during the SATs period! In three of the high-support schools, teachers were older women late in their teaching careers who had expressed anxiety about teacher assessment and were finding or expected to find SATs a difficult task. There was, however, no clear pattern in relation to class organization or number of Y2 children. Three of the five high-support schools had classes which were vertically grouped, with 12–15 Y2 children in each and class sizes of 24–31; the two Y2 classes had 25 and 29 children, respectively.

At the other end of the continuum, six schools had no extra support: in four classrooms, teachers were alone with full classes of 22–28 children while administering SATs (with eight, nine, 28 and 30 Y2 children in each class). All of these, however, received help later (one became well supported, but only after the teacher became ill and 'nearly went under', at which point the head pulled out all the stops to help her). Four schools continued to offer a minimum of support throughout the SATs period in terms of supply or support teachers, active involvement of headteachers, non-contact time and other kinds of support; most of them did offer one or two of these types of support at some point during SATs but the schools were not reorganized and providing support for the Y2 teacher(s) was not generally seen as necessary. What is significant is that only one of these low-support schools had a full Y2 class of 30 pupils; the others were either vertically grouped with small numbers of Y2 children, or team-teaching, as in one case where three teachers had 30 Y2 and 40 Y1 children between them.

In only one school out of 32 did the head not offer any kind of teaching or non-teaching support during the SATs period. This was a vertically grouped class of eight Y2 and 16 Y1 children where a full-time nursery assistant was already present to support a statemented child. This person took the class while the teacher administered the reading SAT in the same classroom.

Thus, high support was usually provided to protect a particularly vulnerable teacher, while low levels of support were likely to be related to school organization. Not only did headteachers vary in the amount of support they offered but also in their attitude towards 'making SATs work'. One headteacher, who was also a moderator, refused to put in support. She felt that SATs should be workable by professionals in a natural situation and did not need the artificial and expensive support so many headteachers were offering; this was said, however, in the context of a competent and experienced teacher, with only eight Y2 children to be tested. There were also those who objected in principle to the idea of SATs and consequently objected to the provision of support to make SATs work. However, these heads also feared for their Y2 teachers if they did not offer support. Support, therefore, was laid on to help the teacher, rather than to ensure the success of the SAT exercise.

Quality of support

The quality of support, especially teaching support, was, understandably, important to the Y2 teachers. In one extreme case the teacher decided to abandon SATs altogether because she felt the support teacher was incapable of handling the rest of the class. Another class teacher felt unhappy about the support teacher's topic work and her way of dealing with it, as well as the support teacher's reference to the class as her own, and her reorganization of it. One school felt that its ancillary was not suitable to be in the classroom and would be used only for clerical duties.

The majority of teachers (24 out of 30) spontaneously expressed concern about the activities of the non-SAT children. In observation we witnessed a wide range of activities, including painting, worksheets, looking for frogs outside, making folders, sewing, cutting out pictures and making peppermint creams. While some teachers had laboriously planned topic work or activities with the supply or support teacher, a few were leaving the curriculum decisions to the covering teacher and expressing concern over their own loss of control. A few also worried about their relationships with children, especially the non-Y2 children in mixed-age classes who had lost day-to-day contact with the teacher. One teacher described deterioration of discipline and lack of care of equipment and felt that his Y1 children were missing contact with and attention from him while he conducted SATs over a five-week period.

Only six teachers said that they were happy about the rest of the class. These teachers commented positively on the quality of the support person: the rest of the class was 'in capable hands', usually while doing a programme of work set by the Y2 teacher him/herself and carried out by the support staff.

Stress in schools

Stress was clearly a major theme: in 25 out of 31 schools headteachers reported stress of some kind in some part of the school. This ranged from mild, general comments about the 'added pressure of SATs' to horror stories about illness and hospitals. We considered who was displaying signs of stress, whether it was our observed and interviewed Y2 teacher, the head, another Y2 teacher, or other teachers in the school. We considered the way stress was reported, whether as general 'pressure', as specific aspects of stress, such as temper, tension or tiredness, or as full-blown, off ill, 'can't cope with anything' stress. We also considered boredom as a factor in stress and demands on time outside of normal school hours. We looked at who reported stress: sometimes headteachers reported stress in themselves or others that we did not observe. Sometimes teachers reported stress in other teachers but not in themselves. Sometimes everybody reported stress in everybody and it was there for all to see.

There was no obvious link between level of stress and amount of support; for example, it was not the case that schools showing high stress had no support or that schools with low stress had a lot of support. While some factors seemed to emerge which identified low-stress schools (small size, headteacher as moderator, withdrawal of children) the same was not the case for high-stress schools. The only pattern seems to be that schools with a lot of support resulting in reorganization and disruption were likely to have a high stress profile.

In half of the high-stress schools, the head was under stress as a result of her involvement with SATs and her attempts to support and protect her teachers. These heads carried out SATs, took the rest of the class while teachers did SATs, sorted out reading books, covered for absent teachers and generally organized all the support they could for the Y2 teachers. The headteacher's stress may have influenced others in the school: one headteacher noticed this herself and claimed that 'there is a leadership problem from me being over-tired, over-stressed, silly or under-tolerant'. ('Never', she added, 'irritable!') Sometimes the head's attempts to help misfired: arranging for support-teacher help before the SATs period, rather than during it, or putting too many adults into a classroom so that managing adults became a burden, did not help the stressed Y2 teachers.

There were eight schools out of 31 for which stress was neither observed nor reported by more than one person and where stress was not an important issue for either the head or the teacher. Four out of these eight low-stress schools were village schools: the number of Y2 children in the school is likely to have helped here, although the number of Y2 children in our observed class does not seem to have been a determining factor. Five of the eight low-stress schools had vertically grouped classes, four of these with Y3, one with Y1 children. The number of Y2 children in the vertically grouped classes varied from two to 20, while there were two Y2 classes with 26 and 30 children, respectively. In three of the low-stress schools headteachers also served as moderators for the LEA. This may have supplied the teachers with extra advice or information and may also have enhanced their confidence if the head and teacher worked together, as was reported in some cases. Because moderating heads were out of their own schools during the SATs periods, Y2 teachers were left to get on with it and may have felt valued by the head's confidence in their ability to carry on independently.

To conclude, we found that, due to the style of assessment, with children having to be assessed individually or in small groups, considerable changes were required to school organization in order to support the class teachers and to cater for the children who were not being assessed. Schools where team-teaching took place and schools where classes were not composed entirely of seven-year-old pupils generally found this task easier; conversely, schools where there were classes made up entirely of seven-year-olds had the biggest task and the most reorganization to effect.

In some schools considerable changes were made to support the administration of the tests and this would generally have a knock-on effect on other staff; where disruption was widespread it contributed to stress within the school as a whole. However, collegial support for the Y2 teachers was the rule rather than the exception, with colleagues offering high levels of support in order to protect them from what was seen as a particularly difficult, stressful and unwanted activity. This support, it should be emphasized, was offered not to enable the assessments to be performed particularly well or quickly, but to support a colleague.

Stress was due not just to the added pressure of work involved in having to do the assessment, but also to the very high level of publicity that the assessments received (an unusual level of publicity at infant school level), and to many teachers' anxiety about formally assessing children as young as this in a way which they felt could label the children. The culture of English primary teachers insists that the assessment of young children should be for diagnostic purposes, and that labelling children is improper, particularly at an age as young as 7 when many children will only have had five full terms of schooling. Teachers are all too well aware of the effect of different lengths of time in the school, different types of pre-school provision, and different family and social backgrounds on children's performance.

Impact on the staff

In the interviews it also became clear that six schools were analysing the SAT experience, asking further questions, and intended to develop practice in some way. Heads and teachers in these schools made both general and specific comments about what they had learned about the teaching/learning dynamic, for example, how their teachers had, in general, improved their powers of observation and their focus on individual needs. This sort of professional development was clearly easier to engender in a school where more than one teacher was involved in the SATs. One of the more exciting schools to visit was a first school where *all* the teachers were involved: the level of participation, discussion and raised awareness was quite marked.

After the 1991 assessment exercise was over, all the heads, except two, discussed the results and the exercise as a whole with their teachers. In five schools there was a tendency to engage in feelings of regret: 'if only the format of the SATs had been better; if only TA [had] been sufficient'. Fullan (1991) reminds us that dwelling on 'if only' is not effective as a strategy for change as it deflects the solution away from the self: the schools which reacted in this way had decided not to use the SAT results as any basis for change. This was in stark contrast to the proactive response of some schools.

The most common pattern of support from our headteachers in the first year of the innovation was to get involved, to lead from the centre of things. Where heads and more than one classroom teacher were involved, or 'in it together', the possibility existed for a collaborative or collegial culture. Ironically, despite the problems with the content of this particular innovation, its size, scope and compulsory nature have led to what we feel can be described as increased collegiality. Teachers traditionally work under conditions of autonomous isolation rather than rich professional dialogue. What we observed in a number of schools was, we believe, the development of what Hargreaves (1994) calls a collaborative culture, rather than contrived collegiality which may be short-lived.

The second time around

SATs were quicker and easier to administer the second year, but this was not always to do with the tests themselves. Some schools had reorganized so that teachers had fewer children to assess. Some teachers had better, rather than more, help in 1992, from heads, colleagues or support teachers, and they saw this as an advantage over the previous year. The amount of support depended on whether there were staff changes, and on how well the Y2 teacher had coped in 1991. There were at least five schools which provided high support, among them one school which also offered high support in 1991. However, the other high-support schools offered far less support, with teachers taking over more SAT responsibility themselves. Several schools gave less support in 1992, but this did not cause difficulties for teachers.

Twelve schools had staff changes, with a new or temporary Y2 teacher in the class during SATs. One school, with five Y2 teachers the previous year, had only one of those teachers remaining. Most of these new teachers were also new to Y2 and had not previously done SATs. New Y2 teachers experienced some of the problems reported the previous year, especially the lack of contact with their class over the SATs period. The new Y2 teachers seemed to benefit from other teachers' SAT experience, especially in terms of organization and support in the school. New Y2 teachers interviewed generally coped well and the stress reported for first-time testers the previous year was not reported at the same level.

Stress

Generally, teachers felt more confident and less stressful about the 1992 SATs. Some were confident enough to adapt SATs they did not like, as with the 'algebra' task:

> Last year we were too frightened to do that . . . we were quite obsessed with sticking to the letter of the law; now this year

we feel more confident and so we change the things we don't like.

Some also felt that having done SATs the previous year enabled them to feel less pressured and more relaxed about what to expect. The more flexible time period helped, too. The highest amount of stress occurred, not surprisingly, in the schools which had staff changes, particularly at Easter. One headteacher felt 1992 had been far worse than 1991 for this reason. The only other stress reported was by heads; teachers reported feeling relaxed and 'more laid back' than the previous year, even those who had found SATs difficult in 1991.

Overall, teachers' reactions to the SATs were still mixed, although the 1992 SATs were generally seen to be less stressful and somewhat quicker to administer than those in 1991. Concerns about disruption of classes remained, as did concerns about the fairness of SATs for some children. The SATs tasks were generally liked and changes to reading were universally welcomed, except for the reading comprehension test. The replacement of the 1991 maths and science 'process' SATs was seen to be in the interest of saving time, although teachers did not, in all cases, feel that much time was saved and some felt the 1992 tasks were not as good because the 'process' element was missing. Although SATs were generally seen to be quicker and easier to administer, many teachers felt that they were not worth doing in terms of the information they gave.

Organization and support

In 1992, over the period March–June, we interviewed 26 head-teachers. The purpose of the interviews was to see how they were managing SATs in 1992 and whether they had made any changes in school procedures in order to accommodate SATs for the second year. It became clear that headteachers were not just confining their responses to how they were accommodating SATs, but also were talking about a number of issues relating to the impact of national assessment on their own practice. It appears that the action taken by headteachers in the second year of SATs varied greatly.

One admitted to doing less in 1992 and being 'less conscientious'. This headteacher was an articulate children's needs ideologist who resisted the change in assessment requirements due to its incompatibility with her philosophy. Some headteachers limited themselves to making only structural changes to aid smoother management of SATs, whereas others began to try to change the culture of the school by looking at issues in teaching and learning. The most proactive headteachers were engaged in both sorts of change and were beginning to analyse the results of national assessment, or to take their local context into account by starting base-line assessments in order to monitor school performance and look to school improvement.

By the kinds of practices the headteachers described, we could classify their actions into three types of change. *Structural* changes included putting in the same support as in 1991, and intentionally moving staff or rearranging the composition of classes. *Cultural* changes included using the Y2 teachers to train others and begin policy writing or, in some cases, where schools were further ahead, to focus collaboratively on some of the key issues in assessment. *Monitoring* involved beginning to look at results to monitor pupil progress. Two of the monitoring headteachers had started a programme of base-line assessments: one was monitoring Y2 maths results and one was analysing her results against the national picture. These heads were in schools where the Y2 teachers in our study were systematic assessors.

Nine schools made structural changes only, 12 made structural and cultural changes, while four schools made all three types of change. One headteacher (in the monitoring group) felt that imposed change is the greatest assurance of innovation and said she had used SATs results after 1991 as a lever to persuade teachers to encourage children to work more independently; she felt she had 'made people work on their own practice'. Another headteacher (in the cultural changes group) used the introduction of national assessment to enforce TA by introducing a once-a-term observation:

> I've made it happen. I made it happen as a directive.

Headteachers' reflections on the first two years

Our questions on national assessment prompted headteachers to talk about the experience of managing multiple innovation. For two years primary headteachers had been the middle managers of many changes, including the introduction of the national curriculum and national assessment, and it seems that this middle position is not always comfortable:

> A head is someone just as buffeted as the teacher by wanted or unwanted and sometimes incomprehensible changes and, what is more, is expected to lead these very changes.
>
> (Fullan 1991)

Ten of our heads expressed the difficulty of being in the middle of the relationship between the teachers and external bodies, such as other schools, the inspectors and the DfE.

Heads found it difficult to manage teachers' sensitivity about feeling 'inspected and tested' and not being treated as professionals. Heads themselves appreciated the commitment of some teachers, saying 'teachers bellyache, then do the best they can', but they also felt that teachers' experience and expertise were being denied because in some cases teachers had given feedback to LEAs and mostly nothing had come of it:

> They never want to know what teachers tell them.

Being in the middle, for one headteacher, meant taking pressure from the inspector for 'not expecting enough' of her children (that is to say, not getting many level 3s).

Sometimes a problem arose out of the transfer of records from first school to junior school. Following the transfer of the previous year's Y2 children, two heads of first schools were experiencing 'poor relationships' with junior schools. Junior teachers did not believe the children's national assessment results. Another difficulty arose over the realization that, in leading the change, the responsibility for INSET, in this case building teachers' assessment skills, lay with the heads themselves:

> We're not taught how to observe, but we've got to develop it.

Suddenly, a major INSET programme on assessment techniques had to be planned and managed at school level. Heads were also dealing with the general resistance of teachers to imposed change. One commented:

> These tests have the stumbling block of being imposed.

The tests were mandatory, she would have to make sure they were done and at the same time cope with the teachers' antagonism. One head tried to lift the guilt that teachers felt about not covering the curriculum during SATs:

> We forgot about the learning for that period: told teachers not to think about anything, just concentrate on SATs.

Another was willing to:

> put curriculum development on hold – I don't want to put additional pressure on teachers.

Some headteachers, particularly intuitives, were resistors themselves, and this caused a prick of conscience in delivering an imposed system. Other heads found a way of feeling less 'in the middle' by becoming moderators and getting more of an 'inside picture' from working closely with the LEA.

Nine of our headteachers implied that they were feeling the effects of innovation overload. It was time for a break in the many changes they were being asked to make. Introducing national assessment was only one of many things on headteachers' minds. One head opted out of helping with SATs because she was in the middle of a pilot appraisal scheme. Two heads of small schools mentioned all the extra work involved in having a class of their own as well as running a school. Catholic school heads were continually involved with liaison with the clergy. Another head foresaw extra work as the role of the LEA decreased. In answer to our question about advice received from the LEA, one head reported sarcastically:

> If the LEA *did* give any advice on choice of SAT or anything . . . it's another piece of paper I haven't read.

Six of our headteachers expressed how change feels threatening and brings a feeling of loss of control. As one put it:

> We are not going to let the government control our philosophy. We've fallen into the trap of being too compliant . . . they are going to dump us with a little bit more.

SATs may be seen as a threat to a headteacher's whole educational philosophy. One head was convinced that her teachers' interpretation of children's performance was right and her criteria for the levels were right. She felt that she intuitively knew what level 3 was, but this was thrown into question when she saw other schools' results. Another felt she had to compromise her philosophy over the choice of SATs: the maths task was chosen as easy to administer, 'not on educational grounds'.

Headteachers expressed a loss of control over the curriculum and uncertainty about the future:

> Other people are setting the agenda, there is flux and insecurity.

One head had:

> sleepless nights about handwriting. Do we do joined-up or not at infant level?

Another looked ahead and found the 'whole issue of Key Stage 2' a worry.

What emerged as a theme from headteachers after the 1992 SATs, was the use of 'contrastive rhetoric' – reaffirming one's own identity by contrasting one's own behaviour and attitudes with those of others (Hargreaves and Woods 1984). The 1992 SATs gave ample opportunities for headteachers and others to indulge in this. One said:

> We've been frank and honest. I know some schools did not test by the book.

One moderator head, who had an overview of several schools, had observed the 'danger of some schools inflating results' and four heads felt disappointed in the integrity of their colleagues. For example, at one school the whole staff

> had spent a lot of time understanding, discussing and interpreting, making sure they had the same standards, doing it properly

and then 'there's all these people getting level 3s everywhere'. And another head asked, rhetorically: 'How could one school have *all* level 3s in one core subject?' These headteachers felt strongly that there was a lack of standardization and some thought that the moderators had not done their job properly; this lack of standardization was disturbing when results are to be published.

There were many other examples of this contrastive rhetoric centring around the 1992 SATs. One LEA adviser felt that local

Y2 teachers must have received better INSET (than those in other LEAs) because 100% of Y2 teachers were able to attend. Another felt they had been fairer and justified English scores which were down on last year as due to 'sticking to the SEAC criteria, whereas others didn't'. A representative from a third LEA felt that others should have been concentrating on assessment as a cross-curricular issue (as they themselves did), but instead were treating subjects discretely which was not good primary practice.

Contrastive rhetoric took the form of pity in three cases, where headteachers felt sorry for the school contexts and working conditions of others:

> The real tension and stress must be in a school where they have no help and where the parents are difficult and demanding.

> We had one visit from the moderator and we are supposed to be a priority school. I hate to think what the others got.

> I wonder what heads do when they haven't the confidence in the teachers that I have?

They clearly believed that some schools suffered lack of support, had inadequate Y2 teachers and were beset by parents putting them under pressure. Others implied that some schools were less organized for SATs and accepted lower standards.

> Standards are important but *whose* will triumph? Comparability between different schools is essential.

> I think some schools interpreted the LEA message as they shouldn't be doing level 4 and the teachers are afraid to try it. I think that's a pity if there are kids who are level 4.

This is similar to the phenomenon described as 'The school down the road (cheats)' – when headteachers refer to other schools where cheating takes place, cannot name these schools specifically, but *know* that it is true (Davidson *et al.* 1993).

Teachers and change

In this section we focus on eight teachers who displayed (in 1991–2) signs of real change in terms of enhanced awareness of assessment methods and purpose. The aim is, first, to describe the developing assessment practices of these eight teachers in response to the introduction of national assessment; and second, to analyse some of the factors which may have contributed to their positive adoption of this major innovation. In accordance with similar findings (Broadfoot *et al.* 1991), classroom observation and interview data indicated that the eight teachers were becoming particularly interested and active in diagnostic assessment. This involved both collaborative and individual assessment practices.

Our eight teachers were instrumental either as school assessment leaders, or within the supportive situation of year teams in instigating discourse about assessment. Elements of such discourse included detailed 'case conference' type discussion of individual children's needs, considerable in-house moderation of pieces of children's work, brainstorming sessions on the issue of open and closed questioning and analysis of the SAT experience. Discussions took place on an informal day-to-day basis and/or during deliberately planned formal staff meetings and allocated non-contact times. On such occasions, our teachers were able to share some of their own individual techniques and strategies.

The eight teachers we refer to considered assessment as a priority. We could also say that these teachers displayed an 'openness' to what evidence of attainment might mean. They were eclectic in their methods of collecting assessment information on children and they appreciated that there were many sources of evidence for assessments. These teachers clearly worked very hard over a prescriptively short period of time on the clerical, administrative and analytic aspects of both TA and SATs. As one teacher put it:

> I have felt it all year, since September. There as been such a big build up to the SATs and so many changes this year. I think the stress now is in relation to all those weeks of worrying about it. I'm just relieved that it's over.

Is this an example of what Fullan (1991) means when he says that one must struggle through ambivalence before one is sure that the new vision is workable and that good change is hard work?

Despite some anxiety, the teachers persevered and maintained a problem-solving stance. The work of Wallach and Kogan (1970) shows that those who report a 'moderate degree of anxiety' are, in fact, most creative in their thinking processes. Indeed, we would like to argue here that all eight teachers demonstrated many of the characteristics of creative thinking:

- they showed a 'freshness of appreciation' (Maslow 1954) when devising assessment techniques;
- they did not necessarily see national assessment, a 'top-down' innovation, as a criticism of their own practice – rather, they were able to see creative potential in solving the problem (Parnes 1970);
- they avoided resisting the change (Moustakas 1967).

Our eight creative teachers came from all four LEAs in the study and received different kinds of INSET and LEA support. It may be significant, however, that three came from the LEA where teachers (from our larger sample) have been particularly appreciative of the INSET they received (see Chapter 5). Some of the other factors we considered and later eliminated in relation to the creativity of the eight teachers were as follows:

- school size – the schools ranged from a 60-pupil village school to a large (300+) multi-ethnic inner-city school;
- catchment area – locations were 'leafy suburbs', metropolitan housing estates, affluent villages, areas of high and low unemployment;
- classroom organization – classes were both mixed-age groups and entirely Y2 classes;
- numbers of children being assessed – this ranged from two to 26 children;
- teacher experience – the group comprised one probationer, one approaching retirement and six in mid-career;
- support – teachers received little or no extra teaching support during SATs.

What, then, were the contributing factors to these teachers' active or creative response to national assessment? The important contextual factors seem to be the role of headteachers and colleagues.

The role of the head in innovation has been the focus of a number of research studies; in the schools of these eight teachers, heads did not impose specific models for assessment. Rather they offered praise, encouragement and moral support to the teachers so that they could develop their own assessment practices. They allowed the teachers to interpret the assessment guidance in a 'writerly', rather than 'readerly' way (Ball and Bowe 1992, after Barthes); in other words, there was room for freedom in interpreting assessment texts. All the heads interacted with the teachers by being 'resource providers' (Smith and Andrews 1989). They organized teaching support, ordered materials, booked rooms, sorted books and took assemblies to provide non-contact time. Four of the heads delegated the implementation of assessment, two so completely that they were unable to discuss the detail of assessment without referring our questions back to the teacher. Another head had delegated assessment to his deputy, while the fourth appointed the Y2 teacher as an assessment co-ordinator. By standing back the heads gave the message that the teacher was trusted to handle assessment competently.

Four of our teachers were working as part of a team of Y2 teachers, each with their own class. The other four were paired in team-teaching situations, sharing a large number of children. What we observed in the schools where these teachers worked was the development of what Hargreaves (1994) has called 'collaborative culture', as already mentioned. This is one of the ideal conditions for real innovation to take place and our observations, supported by the comments of the teachers themselves, suggest that such collegiality during the periods of both TA and SATs allowed the teacher to deal with the challenge of assessment in a positive and professional way. As one teacher said:

We've worked together a lot and it's great to have three of us.

Another teacher, a probationer, referred to the sense of mutual support felt between the three Y2 teachers:

This is an analytical group of teachers and there has been cross-fertilization of ideas.

Thus, despite the problems with the content of this particular innovation, its size, scope and compulsory nature have led, in some cases, to what can be described as increased collegiality. Fullan (1991) shows that the degree of change undertaken by teachers is strongly related to the extent to which teachers interact with each other and those providing help: within the school, collegiality among teachers, as measured by the frequency of communication, mutual support and help, etc., was a strong indicator of implementation success. The benefits gained from this collegiality can be seen as an unexpected and welcome return for effort put in. Indeed, Huberman and Miles (1984) have argued that early rewards are critical incentives to the implementation of an innovation. When talking with these Y2 teachers, it became clear that all felt they had something to gain from actively adopting national assessment requirements. These benefits included an enhanced professionalism and new insights into teaching and learning. These teachers mentioned that they found TA and SATs useful in evaluating their own teaching programmes and felt they could now improve what was on offer to children. One teacher said:

> There are a lot of pointers for our own teaching and it has given us something to aim for.

Another teacher reported:

> I realize we don't do enough talking. I will encourage children to discuss more now, especially in science and speaking and listening.

Teachers also felt they themselves had learned something about learning. One teacher felt he needed to reappraise the part that mathematical apparatus plays in children's learning, and another had learned that the composition of groups and her own classroom management were linked closely to how children learn; she intended to do some personal research during the following academic year.

These teachers were noticeably ready to stand back and reflect on the SAT experience and were willing to recognize that there may be a mismatch between their TA and SAT results. This was in marked contrast to most teachers, who attributed any mismatch to either the format of the SAT itself or to the children's performance on the day. Two of our eight teachers worked as 'change facilitators' (Berman and McLaughlin 1977) to provide a 'change facilitating team' for their schools: both had been delegated the job of implementing assessment in their schools, one as an assessment co-ordinator, the other as an INSET leader.

Thus, we can see that a particular support style from the head could enable teachers to act in a particularly open, creative way. This was clearly not a sole condition for this response, since the picture was far more complex, but it seems an important pointer for empowering teachers.

In summary, the majority of headteachers in the NAPS study got involved in the implementation of national assessment in their schools in 1991 and 1992, either by taking an active role in SATs or by offering support to the Y2 teachers. During the second year, all but one headteacher had made changes (structural or cultural or both) to the way the school was working and four were beginning to monitor pupil progress by analysing their own results. Furthermore, heads' support style appeared to have had a direct effect on the type of response that their teachers developed to the assessment innovation.

5

THE ROLE OF THE LEAs IN MANAGING CHANGE

An important level of support for the school is the local education authority: all our project schools were within LEA control, none had opted out. The support, training and advice which LEAs offer can make a significant difference to how a school approaches and copes with a new programme or policy. In this chapter, therefore, we look at the support offered by the LEA: specifically, what sorts of messages were offered in relation to assessment and how the support offered affected teachers' assessment practice.

The role of the LEA in the implementation of national assessment

> How important district administrators are. What they do at the three main phases of change – mobilization, implementation and institutionalisation – significantly affects the destiny of the proposed change.
>
> (Fullan 1982: 163)

As explained in Chapter 1, we identified four LEAs (described on page 17) in different settings and sought their participation in building up a picture of the introduction of national curriculum assessment at Key Stage 1. After permission was granted from chief education officers, we were referred to LEA personnel who had responsibility for assessment. We interviewed our contacts four times over the period 1991–3. We ended our study at a time when power was shifting from LEAs to schools themselves, and this is inevitably reflected in the data.

This section deals with how the four LEAs mustered forces and battled their way through the first years of national assessment.

Recruitment and mobilization

The four LEAs in our study were gearing up for national assessment as early as 1989, although it did not become statutory till 1991. At this stage they were working somewhat in the dark. As one adviser put it:

> we were working on draft regulations and supposition . . . the first seminars were preliminary, with nobody really getting a clear focus on where they were going. We knew there would be SATs, we knew there would be something called TA, we didn't know where they fitted together.

A consultant working with other LEAs at the time confirms the state a lot of authorities were in – feeling lost, and asking:

> What are the SATs all about . . . what do we need to do?

As time marched on, 'everything started coming to a head' and LEA representatives mustered forces to create assessment teams, attended SEAC briefings and mobilized moderators, LEA staff who were to support teachers and ensure consistency of standards. Over the next three years they mounted their own individual campaigns to support schools, often reconnoitring and changing tactics. From time to time they met with neighbouring authorities who were allies in the cause, to compare notes and discuss strategies.

Creation of assessment teams

One of the first things that LEAs did was to create special assessment teams of advisers/advisory teachers who would deal with

any required training. Across our four authorities, these teams
varied in size, composition and 'brief'.

In Homeshire a team of assessment personnel was set up. Three
members of the team had primary backgrounds. They could not
act autonomously, but had to seek permission from a senior inspector before taking strategic decisions. Their brief was to act as:

> a think tank for policy and training, the creation and training
> of assessment co-ordinators and the production of any train-
> ing documents for use on training days.

Because this was such a large county, the team travelled to four
staff development centres, training key groups. Our key contact at
Homeshire was one of the advisory teachers.

In Midboro, the team consisted of five personnel – one advisor,
three full-time and one part-time advisory teachers who would also
be trainers and moderators. Their brief was threefold: to visit every
school before SATs were done, supply advice and support, provide
INSET for Y2 teachers, heads and any other teachers who may
require it, and analyse city-wide results. Because of the compact-
ness of the city, most of the training was done at the Teachers'
Centre which was easily accessible to all schools. The adviser was
our key contact.

In the absence of any adviser for assessment in Innercity, the
senior primary inspector brought in a consultant from a nearby
university to do the training for SATs. After the first run, a general
inspector for assessment and reporting was appointed. She enlisted
the help of the university consultant again for 1992 and delegated
other training to moderator headteachers. The LEA inspectors and
advisers also supported the schools with school-based INSET and
subject-specific assessment INSET run at the Professional Development Centre. The brief of the inspector for assessment was to look
after primary schools doing assessment at Key Stages 1 and 2 and
to analyse results in order to 'identify what's working and what's
not'. The SATs training was done in style – by booking a large conference centre – but the other training was done at local level by
the moderator headteachers in their clusters and held on school
sites when the children had gone home. This inspector became the
NAPS contact.

Until 1991, the senior inspector in Northshire, along with
other general primary advisers, was dealing with assessment issues.

However, an assessment team of three personnel was set up after the first run when they saw the extent of the training required and the need to analyse results. The team consisted of two moderator headteachers and a research and statistics officer. Their brief was also threefold:

to ensure that teachers' planning was supported by guidance through the mire of stuff that was coming in; to give access to assessment to every single primary teacher;

and to act as co-ordinators to the moderators. The senior inspector's job was to tabulate results. Once again, teacher training was done by the moderators on school sites and in school clusters, whereas the moderators' training days often took place at conference centres. We had interviews with every member of this team, which changed over the years.

Moderators

SEAC had sent out instructions to LEAs and offered training days in 1991. Overall, our four LEAs were not particularly inspired by the SEAC briefings, nor were they pleased about the timing and quality of their publications. (Interestingly, this contradicts the NFER findings (Lee 1993) that 'the majority of respondents found the support provided by SEAC reasonably useful'.)

One of the duties of all LEAs was to decide whom they would appoint to act as moderators; the role of a moderator, generally, is one of ensuring consistency of approach and outcomes in assessment (Harlen 1994). These were crucial strategic decisions because moderators would be working closely with schools at a time of imposed change. In our four LEAs, moderators were chosen internally from different hierarchical layers and this had an impact on how they were perceived in schools.

In 1991, Midboro advertised the post and appointed 'good infant teachers', thus allying moderators with teachers. They chose not to call them 'moderators' at all but 'advisory teachers for assessment'. Because the moderators were teachers they were perceived as non-threatening to both heads and teachers when they went into schools. Homeshire advertised for heads or deputies, implicitly ranking moderators at a higher level than teachers. They were appointed from both mainstream and special schools. Northshire headhunted particular headteachers because of their track record. Innercity went even further up the hierarchy and three inspectors 'were told' they were on the team together with four headteachers who had been elected by their peers. The university consultant for SATs training argued that they should have gone no higher than headteacher level because, by appointing inspectors, real communication with the teachers would suffer. Indeed, the 'helpline', which was set up during SATs time, was underused, possibly because there was an inspector on the end of the telephone and schools may not have wanted to expose their insecurities to him/her. On the other hand, the appointment of inspectors as moderators may have raised the status of the whole process (and the inspector for assessment reported that it proved to have been an invaluable exercise because the primary inspectorate as a whole fully understood the assessment demands on schools).

How the NAPS schools felt about the moderators is explained later in this chapter, but the data shows that in general they played a supportive and problem-solving role in most schools.

As time went on, SEAC asked for more rigorous models of moderation (SEAC 1992) whereby moderators took on a role which genuinely aimed to standardize judgements across schools, rather than simply reassure and support teachers. In 1992, of our four LEAs, only Midboro slightly modified their moderation policy: they advertised internally for 12 volunteers from practising teachers in infant schools. The other three LEAs retained their higher-ranking staff. However, for the third run of SATs, all four LEAs did move towards a more rigorous, accountable model of moderation, following SCAA guidance and renaming the moderators 'auditors' or 'audit moderators' and sending them into schools with more systematic observation schedules. This put more pressure on schools, in Homeshire at least:

> The fact that audit moderators were coming in gave schools an extra fear element.

Training

The approaches of the four LEAs differed quite significantly and this had an impact on the focus of their training (see Table 5).

Table 5 Summary of LEA approaches

LEA	Attitude to national assessment	Responsibility for implementation	LEA roles
Northshire	Positive – to help improve quality of primary education	Shared	Working with schools as leader/partner/regulator
Midboro	Problematic in practice, threatening to espoused philosophies	Adviser's	Protecting schools and records of achievement philosophy
Homeshire	Unwieldy – too difficult	Dispersed	Conveyor of information
Innercity	Useful – to raise expectations	Schools'	Empowering schools, innovator/regulator/banker

Innercity concentrated on training for SATs in 1991 because it was too late to do any TA training, but during the training sessions teachers were given advice on how to gather evidence for TA. Each Y2 teacher had one day's training. In addition, the teachers attended one day of 'SAT familiarization'. The LEA generally encouraged teachers to have a positive attitude to national assessment and told them 'to give it their best shot'. Year 2 teachers also attended one or more after-school sessions with the moderator and other schools in the same cluster. At these sessions, moderators established contact, did agreement trialling and solved any problems.

Midboro offered one and a half days on TA, one day on SATs and half a day after SATs for feedback. Time was spent 'spelling out the legal requirements', albeit 'with a lightish touch', but the main thrust was on agreement trialling when teachers brought in examples from their own classwork and assessed them alongside statements of attainment. Generally, the LEA message was that teachers were legally bound, that they were not to assess by intuition, but to use the criteria; that they were to do their best to collect evidence but to limit the range and quantity. The LEA would be there for advice and support and 'not to be nosy or to police the curriculum'.

Northshire ran some after-school sessions on assessment and classroom management and organization as early as summer 1990. An observation checklist was offered for teachers to try. Two mandatory SAT training days were also given and on these days teachers practised assessing levels from pieces of classwork and were helped to plan for assessment and recording.

The general message from the trainers was:

You've got to do it – you can't avoid it. You've got to see that children are given every chance to achieve.

One feedback day after SATs was optional:

to get positive and negative reactions and to get the emotion out of the way.

Each advisory teacher/moderator had 40 schools and managed to visit each school for half a day before SATs, doing INSET. In all, then, Northshire teachers had the opportunity of attending approximately four to six days' training.

Homeshire training amounted to two days on TA and one on SATs. One other day was given when schools were officially closed and schools were expected to arrange their own INSET programmes in assessment. In 1991 and 1992 training was led by the assessment team, in liaison with other advisory staff. Moderators did preparation for SATs in 1992, using centrally prepared materials. In the training, teachers were advised that Homeshire policy favoured a whole-school approach to assessment and were told that evidence was seen as both tangible work and observation notes. The assessment team passed on the SEAC guidance to their schools and relied on heads and moderators to cascade assessment policy to their teachers. Overall, teachers received three days' official training and some school-led INSET.

In addition to setting up training, the LEAs made decisions about ongoing support for schools. LEA support took the form of extra personnel, helplines and documentation such as assessment packs. Midboro heads were allowed supply cover for teachers on courses, and Northshire and Homeshire offered support to the Y2 teachers in the form of ancillary personnel. For example, in Homeshire, schools were given 10 hours of help from ancillaries to be used at the headteachers' discretion, and in Northshire support teachers were sent into schools for one day per week. Three LEAs (not Northshire) set up a telephone helpline which was used to varying degrees by heads and teachers.

LEAs gave out different messages and advice at very different levels. For example, in relation to the SATs our Innercity schools reported advice on things such as: how to conduct the SATs; which SATs to avoid; giving children the best possible chance; and doing as well as possible. Our Northshire schools reported being advised on who should do SATs in the absence of the Y2 teacher and what kinds of children's comments to accept. Very specific advice was also given by Northshire on most SATs (for example, on science 4, level 1, part c: 'The explanation of the picture overrides the picture itself. Individual oral questioning is necessary. The point of the assessment is that the pupil conveys that light cannot pass through solids' [*sic*]). Midboro teachers had been given advice to retest if in doubt, had been told when to test children as a whole class and had had their own personal observation notes legitimized as evidence; heads had been advised to look at their results as performance indicators. Our Homeshire schools, on the other hand, report very little advice; only one headteacher remembered being advised which SATs to choose.

All of our schools had received advice about assessing children at level 4 in 1992. Midboro and Homeshire did not encourage assessing children at level 4, and teachers had to check their judgements through the LEA. Northshire wanted teachers to give children the benefit of the doubt, but again to double-check. Innercity advised teachers to attempt it and give children the opportunity to achieve. These different approaches, of course, could have had an impact on the LEA performance in the league tables.

Grumbling in the ranks: reactions to LEA training and support

During our first visits and again after the first reported run, we asked trainers, headteachers and Y2 teachers about the support, advice and training on offer. Reactions varied from LEA to LEA and across schools within each LEA.

In Homeshire, the LEA trainers themselves felt that due to a number of local and political concerns, plus the size of the county, the introduction of national assessment had been a problem for them and they had experienced resistance from some headteachers in the particular part of the county visited by the research team. We had 15 respondents from Homeshire schools willing to comment on training, and six of them thought that the training was good, mainly because it confirmed that they were on the right track, or 'it highlighted things we needed to be doing', for example,

> that we were going to need this continuous assessment and we would have to get something into position to keep the children's work as proof.

However, only one headteacher thought the assessment team booklets had been useful. Support came from other sources in the LEA: two headteachers said they had had reassurance from their inspectors. Moderators were part of the assessment team. They were involved in planning the cascade training. Approximately half of our respondents felt supported by the moderators ('she's there for us') and were grateful for their niceness and non-threatening behaviour. However, the others levelled criticisms about relationships ('she treats us like we are thick') and quality control ('she's too easy on children's responses'). Across a wider sample of teachers, the NFER study (Lee 1993: 73) also argued that 'the personality of the moderator was highly influential in determining teachers' views of the support provided'.

The remaining nine of the 16 Homeshire respondents were critical of the LEA training programmes, complaining that the assessment team trainers merely passed problems back to teachers – the cascade model which was perceived as unsatisfactory by the teachers in the NFER study (Lee 1993). Homeshire teachers also felt that the trainers were out of touch with the classroom, that the informal methods did not suit everyone, and generally that 'the LEA didn't know any more than the teachers themselves'. One respondent felt that teachers had been left 'floundering their own way'. The impression from the advisory teacher and moderators was that the Homeshire campaign and the whole exercise of introducing national assessment to schools had been rather unsuccessful and, indeed, only 40% of NAPS respondents felt it had gone well.

The adviser for assessment in Midboro felt encouraged by the fact that only two schools in the whole 'city' had not turned up to the first TA training days in 1991:

> I think my evidence that we've supported people through national assessment is the way in which they have come to training sessions.

He felt that training had gone well, especially the moderation of children's work 'because it brought the classroom to life'. When he received teachers' feedback on the SAT training, he reported that 'there was general agreement that the in-service support was helpful' (Midboro Evaluation of Training document). The NAPS Midboro heads and teachers were more or less split down the middle over their views of the 1991 training. Of our 16 respondents, nine felt that the LEA had been supportive, did not put pressure on them and made them 'more secure'. One headteacher went as far as to say:

> without them I would have gone under. I really take note of what they say.

Teachers had appreciated the moderation exercises done in the sessions, felt they had been taught how to get evidence and had found the information sheets good, 'not theory waffle'. The other seven respondents felt that the training 'came too late', 'was not meaningful' and 'thrust the law' at them. They felt they were not told how to do assessment and most ideas were 'self-generated'. Between 1991 and 1992, six of our headteachers said they felt strongly guided, especially by the adviser. The NFER study (Lee 1993) also showed that 'heads tended to be more enthusiastic about approaches than respondents that were not heads'. It is possible that the heads appreciated the training more than the teachers because it pinpointed their legal responsibilities (which now included 'reporting to parents' – a matter of concern to all heads). One headteacher went as far as to say she was 'literally taken by the hand and taken through'.

In 1991, 12 of our 16 respondents thought the moderators had been 'quite helpful' and had 'tried to make it less onerous' by giving good suggestions. There was general approval of the moderators being infant teachers ('at least no secondary people thrust upon us') and of their credibility ('she knows what she is talking about').

At the end of our study, the adviser was battle-weary. He felt that, although the imposed system of national assessment had helped the LEA advisers to sharpen up assessment as an integral part of teaching and that consequently practice in some schools had improved, the whole exercise had not been easy. He was ambivalent about the success of the Midboro campaign, and so, it seemed, were the NAPS schools (56% approved of how it was handled). On the other hand, the adviser felt that some teachers were certainly moving towards assessing or already assessing against criteria and he believed that bringing teachers together had been the most useful aspect of the enterprise and this was echoed by other LEAs throughout England and Wales (Lee 1993).

There was no assessment adviser in Innercity in 1991, and consequently there was a delay in sorting out the introduction of national assessment. This meant that the training for TA and SATs was combined over two days. The consultant, brought in as an *ad hoc* measure to deal with SATs, reflected on the training she had given to Y2 teachers and felt that 'the SATs familiarization days were the most important things', and this had been confirmed by teachers talking to moderators. The small amount of early training in TA was widely felt to be a disadvantage.

All 17 respondents had something to say about the moderators (who were either headteachers or inspectors). They were clearly approved of by 12 of our contacts because they were 'helpful', 'seemed very happy', 'paid regular visits and gave reassurance' and 'their role has been to alleviate insecurities about levels'. One headteacher went as far as to say:

No teacher in Innercity is doing SATs completely on her own – no one needs to feel isolated.

The other five made complaints such as 'advice came after the event' or 'they're taking too lenient a view – trying to ensure Innercity results come up'. In Innercity, then, moderators were seen as significantly more useful and supportive than either training or LEA packs for schools.

In the first year Innercity had had to resort to *ad hoc* measures for training. During the second year, when the adviser took command, she was in favour of devolving power to individual schools and believed that headteachers should stand on their own feet and plan their own school-based INSET. This was supported by inspectors and advisers running staff meetings in schools and also by some centrally provided courses on whole-school policies for assessment and subject-specific assessment training. However, the heads and teachers in the NAPS schools may have seen this passing of power as a lack of support (only 33% approved of the training and the LEA packs). By the end of our study the adviser maintained that the:

> Authority had worked very hard to support schools in the changes imposed by central government, particularly national curriculum and associated assessment requirements.

The best thing they had done was to send local league tables of results to schools, because this had encouraged headteachers to take charge and look at ways of improving their results which, in turn, had led to a:

> sea change in primary schools – a significant shift in thinking about the role of assessment it teaching and learning.

In 1991, the senior inspector for primary education in Northshire explained that her plan of campaign, her approach to training, would be holistic, that assessment training would fit within a general move to improve the quality of education overall, and the focus would be on issues such as classroom organization and the management of teaching and learning. Back in 1990, she had run some after-school sessions. She had been generally pleased with the turn-out, but discovered the change issues quite early on. First, teachers maintained they had always done assessment: 'It was the old view of course: "we are doing it all the time"'. Second, teachers resented the imposed system, seeing it as a challenge to their judgement: 'The jump from the intuitive to getting them to be more objective was a big step'. Third:

> they were also having to break new ground in so far as they were talking about practice in more depth, and that is threatening.

Fourth, some teachers were:

> anti, because there was so much unknown. The actual SATs and the media weren't helping. Mrs Thatcher, at the time, saying 'pencil and paper tests' – well, all of that was working against what we were trying to do.

Clearly, then, it was no easy task, in those early days, for Northshire trainers to fit assessment developments within 'whole-county planning' on school improvement. As time went on, throughout 1991 and 1992, inspectors and link advisers were involved 'all along the way' in the training programme and in 1992 all training was oversubscribed. The assessment team was confident that it was offering appropriate training to heads and teachers.

All eleven respondents in Northshire schools had something to say about the LEA support systems and the training (which was actually carried out by the moderator headteachers). Only one headteacher complained that the LEA were reactive, not proactive. The other ten respondents really appreciated the LEA campaign. Training went down well. Heads liked it when the LEA interpreted SEAC documents for them, and teachers liked interpreting statements of attainment and moderating examples of work, or, as they called it, 'doing real grading'. (This is corroborated in the NFER study (Lee 1993) which found that the preferred approach was for small groups of teachers to work together on practical tasks.) They also appreciated 'a very useful checklist for classroom management during SATs' and 'a potted list of SoAs you could carry around'. One headteacher went as far as to call the training 'excellent – doing SATs was good!'. For the most part, our Northshire headteachers felt supported by the LEA. The creation of support teachers was welcomed:

> the process of SATs would have been much more haphazard, less controlled and more traumatic, if not for the [support time] from the LEA.

Eight of the 11 respondents in Northshire mentioned the support given by the moderators when they came into schools. They were found to be 'very sympathetic and approachable', 'understanding, not inspectorial' and were seen to 'make positive inputs into schools by clearing up difficulties'. This view is echoed in the NFER study which found that 'it was easier for moderators to satisfy teachers' expectations if their role was seen as trouble-shooter'. (Lee 1993: 73) By the end of our study the Northshire assessment team were feeling quite satisfied with the way in which they had introduced national assessment. Their training had been generally appreciated by the schools and their teachers were showing a growing realization of what counts as evidence. Over 40 headteachers had signed up for Key Stage 2 training in the coming year.

Discussion: satisfaction and LEA characteristics

Of all LEA training campaigns, the Northshire campaign was most appreciated by its recruits – 91% of our respondents felt it went well, while in Innercity only a third felt this; in Midboro approval was at 56%, and in Homeshire 40%. When we looked at opinions about perceived support from the moderators, the picture is slightly different, with Midboro teachers voicing marginally more feelings of support than Northshire, with 75% and 72% of respondents feeling supported respectively, while 70% of Innercity respondents and only 52% of Homeshire respondents felt supported.

The ways in which our four LEAs supported their schools through the introduction of national assessment seem to be based, for the most part, on how they saw the innovation, how they saw themselves as change agents and how they saw the teachers who were to be the 'users'.

The attitude to national assessment (the innovation) in Northshire was that it should be 'a learning experience for everybody'. It was everyone's responsibility. All those involved saw themselves as part of a whole-county team of inspectors, primary advisers, assessment advisers, heads and teachers. For this reason, they preferred that the research team interviewed as many LEA representatives as possible – they wanted to present a consolidated response. Developing expertise in assessment was not seen as a bolted-on requirement, but as an integral part of an overall county plan to improve primary education. Perhaps because of this, they headhunted moderators from heads whom they recognized as running good primary schools, because, as moderators, they would be doing a considerable amount of training and giving inputs at cluster meetings. These meetings were likely to touch upon fundamental issues of philosophy as well as assessment, and the LEA hoped that by a kind of osmosis good general practice would spread.

This whole-county approach was followed through by stressing that Y3 teachers should 'use and believe in the results' sent up by colleagues and also by training Y1 and Y6 teachers and heads in junior schools. In addition, monitoring and evaluation procedures triangulated opinion from all levels involved in assessment and, as part of these procedures, individual school results, compared to county-wide results, were to form the basis of discussion between heads and their link advisers.

Northshire advisers recognized that 'generic assessment' was going on in classrooms and 'knew that the teachers were good'. They felt that their role was to 'ensure those teachers had guidance' through the implementation of national assessment. The LEA took a collegial stance to the heads and teachers and made it possible for them to feel supported, while leaving them to make some of the decisions for themselves. In other words, responsibility for implementation was shared by all those participating. A set of documents was designed by the LEA and was highly approved and used by heads and teachers. Very specific advice on each SAT was sent into schools to guide the smooth administration of SATs and the moderator heads were there for emotional back-up. The LEA designed a specific format for reporting results to parents and most schools adopted the format which stressed national curriculum attainment and pupil targets and paid less attention to achievement issues.

Northshire LEA took a positive attitude to national assessment: 'You've got to see that children are given the best possible chance'. For this reason, it encouraged teachers to attempt level 4s (and a few did). In addition, it aimed at the enhanced professionalism of teachers – 'There's bound to be a diagnostic outcome of what's happening' – by producing a document for schools which suggested ways in which they could use the national assessment results. The advisers saw themselves as 'planting seeds for planning and policy' and encouraging schools to be diagnostic about why their results were as they were. Within its whole-county plan, the Education Committee is currently considering the results as part of a review of admissions procedures and funding for nursery education.

Overall, Northshire LEA took a positive stance towards the implementation of national assessment and a collegial attitude to its schools, sharing the responsibility with all those involved. Assessment was seen as one crucial aspect in developing the whole curriculum. The LEA played a threefold role of 'Leader-Partner-Regulator' (Audit Commission 1989) by articulating a vision of what it was trying to do, supporting schools and helping them fulfil the vision while, at the same time, regulating the quality of the schools' work.

The Midboro adviser saw the introduction of national assessment as problematic, particularly because it was imposed from above:

> the principles of assessment are right but the arrangements are not modelled on the reality of what schools are really like.

What looks good in print is actually very difficult to bring about.

Because he felt that the government did not understand life in classrooms, he was very keen to manipulate both information and training into something teachers would find useful and relevant. He saw his role as 'interpreting and personalizing' the DES/SEAC messages and making them user-friendly:

> I do not believe that Y2 teachers have the time available to read it all . . . At least I've got the flexibility and I'm supposed to make time to do this. It's a different kind of use of the brain that's required for class teaching and lesson preparation and organization. You can't expect people to suddenly switch on to Circular 8/90.

LEA training for TA took a kind of teacher-centred approach by 'bringing the classroom to life' through using teachers' interests and biographical anecdotes and offering hands-on experience and role play. Teachers were sympathetically told to 'do their best' when it came to SATs. The LEA recording format was that of a record of achievement and the adviser saw part of his role as 'persuading schools to include other things about children beyond levels and ATs'.

The adviser recognized, however, that the government's philosophy was different:

> There has been a tremendous investment in assessment that is summative . . . end of key stage based around standard tests. I think that there has been such an investment of money and philosophy that I can't believe it will be lost. But people will see that it could have been used somewhere else.

The adviser saw national assessment as something that would worry teachers and felt that part of his role was to allay their fears by means of a softly-softly approach:

> I believe that if teachers are frightened, they won't share their understandings or misunderstandings so we try to be always at the end of a phone.

Determined that 'nothing would come as a surprise' to Midboro teachers, the adviser shouldered most of the responsibility for the implementation of the assessment procedures himself. For example, Midboro teachers could not make decisions about level 4 without consulting the LEA. However, almost half of the Midboro teachers felt they received little real advice on how to do assessment or how to use results. Mostly, they felt they were given legal updates, although this was appreciated by headteachers.

The introduction of national assessment in Midboro appears to have been treated as a separate issue and not meshed into any general plan for primary education. The creation of assessment co-ordinators in schools could be seen as an (unintentional?) move to make assessment a specialized issue. Overall, the adviser for assessment took a proactive stance towards the assessment and a protective stance towards his schools conveying instructions from SEAC, while at the same time sensitizing teachers to the pitfalls of national curriculum assessment. His role was a dual one of 'conveyor-defender' (Havelock 1969) and 'hero-innovator' (Audit Commission 1989).

In the NAPS project, our Homeshire contact was an advisory teacher in the team of assessment personnel. This section, therefore, deals with the data relating to *her* involvement in the introduction of national assessment and, as such, may not represent the LEA as a whole. The national assessment structure was seen from the outset as too unwieldy and difficult to manage for the average classroom teacher. The team saw assessment as a cross-curricular issue, to be addressed within general national curriculum training, but the advisory teachers found it very difficult to mesh in assessment training because of local relationships between the different groups and hierarchies involved in the advisory structure of Homeshire. For example, they were never sure they were given credibility by the inspectors.

The main issue was about where the authority lay to make ultimate decisions. There were certain decisions the team could not take and because decisions were constantly delayed, schools were often given very short notice and often reacted to that. Responsibility for the implementation of national assessment was fragmented and assumed to lie with a number of people – the senior inspector for staff development, Curriculum Planning Committee, subject advisers, heads of staff development centres, the assessment team. As an outcome, there were 'conflicting and separate messages from different sources going into schools'. Schools were receiving different bits of information from different sources, (for example, 10 hours' ancillary help from LEA administration, pressure to collect evidence and assessment documents from the assessment team, an imposed record-keeping format from the inspectorate, training for SATs from the moderators, advice to check their judgements about level 4 from the inspectors) and there appeared to be no cohesive policy offering a united approach. Perhaps due to the lack of a clear cohesive county policy, the eight NAPS schools (and remember, there were only eight) were critical of LEA advice and training (a cascading model dependent on heads, assessment co-ordinators and moderators). More than half felt generally unsupported and thought the LEA had 'passed the problems back to the teachers'.

The role adopted by the trainers in the assessment team appears to be that of the 'conveyor' described by Havelock (1969), that is, of government agent bringing the DfE orders to schools: 'we were obliged to tell about the statutory requirements, we were obliged to give training'; 'we were doing what we were supposed to do'. For example, in level 4:

> We gave them the SEAC advice which was to enter pupils if they saw fit.

This was clearly not an acceptable role to the NAPS schools, and indeed those in the team found the area in which the NAPS research was conducted to be 'full of resisters' and had experienced 'a sort of antagonism'. Overall, the assessment team members saw national assessment as problematic for themselves and their schools and they were limited in the responsibility they could take in its implementation.

As a former district of the Inner London Education Authority, Innercity was probably ahead of the game as far as assessment was concerned. The PLR, in place for a number of years, had engaged teachers in diagnostic assessment and in reporting to parents. Perhaps for this reason, less stress was placed on training in TA. Nevertheless, Innercity 'has all the difficulties of an inner-city area' and the LEA was keen that socio-economic factors should not become an excuse for performing poorly on national curriculum tests.

The LEA felt that some schools had become resigned to the fact that inner-city schools could not be expected to get high scores and so national assessment was seen as a process which would 'knock some of the complacency away'. Teachers were told 'to give it their best shot' and to offer children the best possible chance, including level 4. In addition, the LEA intended to use national assessment results to argue for more funds – a value-added analysis of school results would help it 'identify what's working and what's not'. National assessment was seen within the context of the Education Reform Act and the resulting shift of power to heads and governors: the LEA role was to empower teachers and to do everything they could to allow heads to fly the nest and 'move away from the paternalistic security of the LEA'. Schools were to be regarded as 'competent and professional' and the LEA technique was to present schools with suggestions and let them choose. For example, guidance documents were sent to school to be used if schools so decided and headteachers could buy a pad of LEA-designed report cards and pay for it from their delegated budget. Similarly, in the case of level 4, schools could make their own decisions and the LEA would trust them:

> If there were any chance of a child gaining this level, the school should be encouraged to do level 4 and we would not be requiring extra proof or evidence.

Training and moderation were characterized by delegation – there was a bought-in consultant for SATs; moderator headteachers did the INSET; and schools which had experience in the pilot were listed as points of contact for schools with queries; Innercity headteachers had nominated their peers and hence delegated the powers of moderation. The LEA provided various assessment courses, and inspectors and advisers delivered school-based assessment INSET at the request of headteachers. Responsibility for implementation and school improvement was devolved to schools by means of Innercity's own internal league table which ranked schools in order of success and in such a way as to show that socio-economic circumstances did not necessarily account for poor scores. Overall, the LEA appears to have sought to empower its schools. National assessment was seen as one issue about which schools could make their own decisions, but also as an opportunity for schools to review their own results and expectations. The role played by the LEA was innovative because it initiated diffusion in schools, but also acted as 'regulator-banker' (Audit Commission

1989) by trying to ensure quality in schools by channelling funds to enable schools to deliver.

Teachers and the LEA

How did the support offered by the LEA affect teachers' assessment practices? We argued earlier, in Chapter 2, that intuitives had made least changes to their everyday practices, evidence gatherers had made little change beyond collecting evidence, and systematic planners had made most changes by introducing assessment sessions into everyday work. We were interested to see if there was any link between the LEA support and the teachers' assessment practices.

When we looked at the different models of TA that we had identified over 1991 and 1992, our sample teachers in Homeshire consisted of four intuitives, one teacher combining the practices of intuitive and evidence gatherer, while the other three teachers were evidence gatherers. (In addition, two other teachers who were not key NAPS teachers, but who contributed to the project, combined the practices of evidence gathering and using intuition.) Why was Homeshire characterized by these two TA models?

Both of these groups had made little change to existing practices. During 1991 and 1992, the eight Homeshire schools in the NAPS study had shown resistance to national assessment during the training and had not felt particularly supported by the LEA. (They did, however, report feeling more supported in 1993 when the team had been reformulated.) The schools felt that in 1991 and 1992 there was a lack of communication through conflicting messages and, of course, no amount of good thinking by itself will address the problem of faulty communication where a desired change is concerned (Sarason 1972: 206). This could be why some Y2 teachers clung to intuition and resisted assessing in relation to criteria. On training days, stress had been placed on the collection of evidence, and some other teachers had clearly picked up that evidence was important and hence became evidence gatherers. By 1992, we had identified no systematic planners in Homeshire (and no teacher had aligned themselves with systematic planning):

> Even when the source of change is elsewhere in the system, a
> powerful determining factor is how administrators take to

change. If they take it seriously the change stands a chance of
being implemented. If they do not, it has little chance of going
beyond the odd classroom.

(Fullan 1991: 197)

Although the assessment team members took the change seriously
and relayed the DfE requirements to their teachers, they felt that
they were not in a position to give schools advice (for example, on
how to go about day-to-day TA). Homeshire relied heavily on the
cascade method of training, and this was perceived as unsatisfactory
by many teachers nationally (Lee 1993). From the outset the LEA
had seen the national assessment structure as unwieldy and too
difficult for teachers to accommodate. This message could have
implicitly reached teachers and hence change took the form of
simply collecting pieces of evidence to back up practice which
remained virtually unchanged.

In Innercity, the picture was slightly different. In 1991–2 we
had identified four systematic planners (including two in a team),
one teacher with the practices of both evidence gatherer and
systematic planner, one evidence gatherer and three intuitives. Thus
all three models were present, but there was a slight leaning towards
systematic planners. LEAs have been known to set schools learning
goals and stimulate progress by linking activities and performance
data to improvement criteria (Laroque and Coleman 1989, cited in
Fullan 1991: 207). Innercity LEA did this and had implied that TA
and testing were useful tools to raise expectations. They sent local
league tables to schools to prompt some action. It may be that some
teachers saw ongoing assessment as a way of raising standards or
of improving on results, and so they had taken to using systems.
Moderator headteachers could also have played a part in influencing
the uptake of systematic planning. Certainly one of our eight headteachers led her own school towards this model of TA. At the
same time, the LEA had 'let go', leaving it up to schools to handle
the innovation in their own ways – inevitably they did, hence all
three models were represented.

By 1992 in Midboro we had identified four systematic planners,
three evidence gatherers and one intuitive teacher. Systematic planners had made most changes to everyday practice. The development
of systematic assessment in Midboro schools may have been due

to the system set up by the LEA. The adviser believed in using the credibility of practising teachers and so he trained assessment co-ordinators and appointed 'real' Y2 teachers as moderators, both of whom would cascade information back into schools. They stressed that teachers should not be relying on intuition and kept pulling them back to assessing against criteria. In two cases our systematic planners were assessment co-ordinators, and in the other two the headteachers were involved in working parties for assessment at LEA level. Headteachers reported great faith and trust in the LEA adviser who seemed to have frequent personal interaction with them – this is the key to implementation of a change (Fullan 1991: 199). For example, he was willing to take meetings at their schools. He communicated well with headteachers regarding the legal requirements, and they clearly felt supported. He probably had most influence over heads while the moderators had most influence over teachers, but the whole package meant that assessing against criteria, as systematic planners did, had a good chance of success.

Northshire's data showed three evidence gatherers, three systematic planners and two intuitives, so all three models were represented. No single model of TA had been 'sold' by the LEA because it believed in generic assessment and that its teachers were good (i.e. at doing assessment). In addition, advisers were constantly changing – a factor that often works against change (Lee 1993: 85) – and this may have meant that advisers offered something for everyone. The LEA directed its energies to influencing the entire school culture towards collaborative planning and whole-school policy for assessment other than targeting individual Key Stage 1 teachers' practice (and the assessment documents produced by the LEA were not prescriptive but to be dipped into at the school's discretion). Moderator headteachers were headhunted because they were felt to run a good school and were fully appreciated by our eight schools, but their philosophies and hence their influence could have been different.

This chapter has described how the four LEAs differed in the ways they appointed assessment personnel and consequently in the kinds of training, advice and support that they were able to offer schools. From the data collected from our 32 schools (eight in each LEA), we could see that some Y2 teachers were satisfied with the training for

TA and with the support and advice for SATS, while others clearly were not. However, most teachers really appreciated the support of visiting moderators. LEA advisers' attitudes to national assessment itself and to the responsibility for its implementation varied. This may have led to the adoption of different roles by LEA advisers and to different reactions to change and to the adoption of different models of TA by the Y2 teachers.

6

USE OF RESULTS

Use of results outside the school

Concerns about publication

During the first visits to schools in spring 1991, headteachers were asked what use they expected would be made of national assessment results. This brought an emotional response from many, concerned overwhemingly with what they regarded as the 'frightening prospect' of publication.

While all of the 32 headteachers expressed disapproval of publication, three made it clear that they would refuse outright:

> I shall tell them *no*, under no circumstances will I publish those results. I don't care if the rest of the county do.

Two of these three carried out the SATs that year, but did not submit the results to their inner-city LEA, which incurred government displeasure for collecting very few results. The third school withheld results from the LEA until the last possible moment, but eventually capitulated.

Only one headteacher, while against publication, could find any advantage to it:

> data concerning schools that are achieving then become available to other schools to investigate why.

Before the 1992 results were published, 26 of the headteachers were again asked (in interview) what they felt about this new requirement to publish. Although the majority remained opposed, there was some evidence of mellowing.

The two headteachers who were generally positive about the idea of all schools publishing results both had good results, at least in relation to expectations for the area:

> I am not worried: this is a good school.

Six headteachers appeared to accept the orders to publish, rationally, if reluctantly:

> The suggestion is that we publish a joint report across all the local schools, contextualizing the results. I think that's what we'll do. We'll ignore it as much as possible and then, when we have to, we'll deal with it jointly.

Two of these six 'accepting' headteachers, who had large ethnically mixed schools or schools in lower-income areas, were working towards the introduction of 'value added' in relation to published results. They had each already started planning base-line assessment profiles of children.

The remaining 18 headteachers still maintained their hostile stance, in some cases the anger having hardly abated:

> I hate the idea of testing seven-year-olds and pinning your results to your front gate.

These headteachers were particularly concerned at the use others would make of the results, especially politicians, the media, LEAS, governors and parents. The particular reasons given related to expectations that:

- school comparisons would not be 'fair';
- comparisons would lead to increased competition between, rather than collaboration with, neighbouring schools;
- emphasis on accountability would be at the expense of educational aims.

Comparison, competition and the LEA

Some headteachers were not opposed to local accountability, but only to general publication:

> The parents should know and the LEAs would have the results anyway, it's just the publishing of results that worries me.

Headteachers were generally suspicious of the unfair use of the results by government as 'political capital' and 'propaganda' to castigate schools, teachers and LEAs.

Ten of the 1991 respondents volunteered their fears that schools would be compared by the media, by politicians, or simply by local people, on the basis of raw scores, without taking social context into account:

> Raw number scores could be frightening if they are not set within a context.

> The context in schools and children's home life won't matter when it comes to media reports. It will give messages to children, the parents, the community, politicians and teachers. Some parents will say 'I told you that school was no good'.

Headteachers in inner-city schools were particularly concerned as they expected that their results would compare unfavourably with those of other LEAs; and they were right, with Bradford, which came out at the bottom of the LEA league table, being pilloried in the press (*Times Educational Supplement*, 1993).

> The class thing comes into it. The kids here are inner-city kids. They have less experience, whilst kids in [Homeshire] who would be more used to it would enjoy it.

Some headteachers in more prosperous areas expressed sympathy with their colleagues:

> I don't think it's going to give a national picture. How can someone in [Innercity] be doing the same with their seven-year-olds as we're doing with ours? They have different backgrounds . . . it can't be the same.

(Interestingly, the 1991 results from our set of case-study schools, picked randomly in each of these two contrasting LEAs, showed surprisingly little difference.)

Although most headteachers expressed confidence that they had the support of their parents, and thus did not fear any local comparisons, three schools voiced a fear of local competition. These were all heads of small schools, and two were worried about impending closure. In 1992, seven headteachers (although none from Homeshire LEA) mentioned that the LEAs would be likely to use results to 'keep tabs on schools with very low levels'. Headteachers in Innercity were most likely to worry about the use their LEA would make of results. One headteacher feared that she would have:

> the LEA breathing down our necks because national standards may not be reached here.

Few headteachers felt that results would be used positively by the LEA. Interestingly, one headteacher felt that her LEA 'won't be terribly interested' because 'they are much more trusting and laid back than other authorities'. This LEA, she explained,

> make no artificial demands, they have more interest in equal opportunities and community.

In Northshire LEA three headteachers felt that the results could be used by the school, or by the LEA, to justify resources. The LEA 'will now look at the quality of [its] provision in the light of assessment'. The head of a school in a deprived area of this LEA felt that his school's poor results could be used to argue for the financial support he needed from the LEA:

> I hope the LEA will make some use of the results to the benefit of schools like this. . . . We can say we have very poor children. We have poor results. We have a case for . . . extra financial support. That is the only way that we are going to get it.

Parents and children

One of the main concerns of respondents, both heads and teachers, was how national assessment results would be used by parents. Some felt that parents would have little interest in the results:

> The question about all these tests is, who are they for? Parents only really want to know if the child is happy at school.

> Even in this middle-class catchment area parents are not particularly interested in knowing whether their child is level 2.

They are really interested in that child's very specific progress, not a level that they don't understand.

Parents who have mentioned it are mainly teachers. Not one of the others asked anything about the national curriculum or national assessment.

Some headteachers felt that parents in their schools would not be able to understand results, in one case because of parents' own lack of literacy. Two other headteachers felt that parents, being unable to understand them, would be 'frightened' or 'terrified' of the results. Overall, six respondents felt that parents would be 'confused' or 'worried' by the numbers:

The secret garden of education was just beginning to come open to parents and they were getting to grips with it. Now, with new jargon, things like 'profile components', it has become not only a secret garden, but an absolute secret jungle.

While arguing that parents would either not understand or not be interested in results, respondents at the same time feared that parents would make misguided use of the results. More specifically, some headteachers feared that parents would confuse national assessment results with their own experience of testing, namely the 11-plus:

It may seem to parents like the 11-plus, which is a test to be passed or failed. Parents may feel that a child is failing.

There was, for example, a feeling that parents would expect children to make steady progress through the national curriculum by going up a level each year, although teachers recognized that 'some children won't achieve level 3 ever'. Some respondents were worried about the media 'whooping up parents'. One effect would be that the parents' desire to see progress would eventually put pressure on junior and middle schools:

[Homeshire] parents are very astute and will want to see pro-gress when they get their second report.

Parents will want to know the levels at Key Stage 2 and will be very anxious if children are still on level 2.

A second expected outcome was that parents would use results to compare schools to 'decide if it is a good or bad school'. Ultimately, some feared that parents might use results 'to shift children from school to school', looking for a school with better results.

There was also the fear that parents might put the blame on teachers or schools for poor results:

> Parents will like being given levels and numbers, but if they [are] disappointed with their child's level, they will blame the school.

> Parents will say that teachers aren't doing their job properly when a child doesn't move up a level each year.

Here again, the context of the school and the children's social background was a concern, as respondents felt that they would be judged and blamed if a child was seen to be under-achieving.

So, overall, many respondents feared that some parents would not understand national assessment results and that others would use the results to compare schools and then to blame schools or teachers if results were poor. Fears that parents would compare children against each other were centred around the most vulnerable children whose results showed them at level 1 or working towards level 1. Thirteen respondents felt that parents would want to see progress and would be likely to put pressure on children to achieve:

> It won't be encouraging. Parents [will] stand in the playground comparing which book children are on. Pressure will be put on children who aren't able to cope.

> Parents will become aware of levels and make comparisons. They will boast about a level 3 child and keep their mouths shut if their child is level 1.

One headteacher felt that parents might find it difficult to accept levels for their children which were 'hard-hitting, but truthful':

> Some parents are very pushy and have high expectations for children at age 7. Parents may put their own pride into a child's achievement.

The strongest statements about the effects on children centred on the wrongness of 'labelling' seven-year-old children with national assessment levels:

The media are simplifying things for parents into:
1 – below average
2 – average
3 – above average.
It's not a good thing to label a child, even at above average, for reasons of motivation and achievement.

Labelling seven-year-olds with results is divisive for children, especially for some who will say 'I'm at level 3'.

Some clearly felt that children should be protected from knowing their national assessment results:

Reporting can do a lot of damage to children, if the child begins to feel that the parents only love him or her by what is achieved.

Concern was expressed about:

the competition of levels and children knowing which books and which levels they are on.

One headteacher summed up the opposition to the pressure put on children, which was seen to be created by the use of results:

Children will have their childhood taken away from them with all this pressure.

Thus, before the first round of Key Stage 1 assessment in 1991, headteachers saw little use for results within schools. Even before publication in 1992, with the exception of a few optimists who felt that poor results might help to bring in extra help for children or schools in need, no positive uses of the results were envisaged. Concerns centred around the publishing of results in the media, without taking into account the social contexts of school and backgrounds of children. It was felt that such 'league tables' would lead to comparisons of results by parents and LEAs, with blame attributed to teachers and schools where results were poor. The outcome of this situation could be children being moved between schools where results were better, or pressure put upon children to achieve, either by parents themselves, or by schools who felt pressured into 'teaching to the test'.

Speculation about the use of results was therefore generally negative, with little reference to the improvement in education quality which results were intended to provide. In particular, the schools were expressing their determination to resist the additional pressure to achieve which the government was trying to exert.

A damp squib: reporting in 1991 and 1992

It seemed likely that the attitude of headteachers to the results would affect their decisions about communication of results. Hence reactions from within the schools will be summarized briefly before we go on to describe to whom results were sent and the nature of the feedback from outside the school.

In 1991, headteachers' reactions varied in intensity; some were very pleased or 'bitterly disappointed', others apathetically dismissive of SATs as only confirming the results of teacher assessment. (In fact, our data suggest that in most of the latter schools the perception was not entirely justified.)

Of the four headteachers who were disappointed, one was 'frustrated' and 'embarrassed' that the results did not show children's real ability, but the other two were concerned about their results only in comparison to those of other schools. Both these headteachers defended their own school's integrity; one, reflecting on what she had seen in other schools in her capacity as a moderator, regretted that her teachers had been 'scrupulously fair' and hence had undermarked.

In 1992 the 15 headteachers who were pleased with the results said that this was because they were similar to or better than the previous year. Four of these headteachers wanted to stress how much progress the children had made and regretted that this was not always reflected in the way results were reported (for example, in the case of SEN children). The seven headteachers who were not pleased with some or all of their results said that this was because they were either worse than or had not been an improvement on the 1991 figures. Poor results and lower scores were attributed, in some cases, to the abilities of the 1992 cohorts of children who were 'very different from last year' or to SEN children's results 'pulling down all scores'. Seven heads persisted in their belief that the results told them nothing new.

In general, then, it can be seen that headteachers were mostly either satisfied or pleased with the results. In 1992, in contrast to 1991, most comparisons were ipsative, that is to say with the school's previous results, rather than with those of other schools or any real or ideal national 'standard'. There was some feeling in both years that number and reading standards were set too high and those for science too low.

Schools had been told in 1991 that results would not be reported since it was the first national run of assessment at the end of Key Stage 1. However, this policy was later changed by the government, and although individual schools were not required to publish results, LEAs were required to collect them for all their schools and forward them to the DES. Not surprisingly in the circumstances, some headteachers were reluctant to send their results to the LEA, and some LEAs did not insist on returns in such cases. The DES compiled a league table of LEAs, showing the percentages of results at each level in each subject. Although some percentages were based on partial data, the table was widely published in national newspapers. Both national and local papers highlighted the poor performances of the lowest-scoring LEAs, with often little consideration of the circumstances of the schools or pupils. Some headteachers felt betrayed by their local press and its 'teacher bashing'.

> We were sold down the river . . . told it was a pilot and they publish the results.

It was not clear to all teachers and heads to whom results were meant to be sent, so that the distribution of 1991 results varied widely. One teacher articulated this confusion:

> We had a day to analyse everything at the end of it and we said, 'Who are these going to?'. Nobody seemed to know. We said, 'What are we going to do with all this information now?'. It was all loose ends. So we put them in the cupboard, where they stayed until yesterday [when the researchers were due to visit].

In 1992 reporting mechanisms were changed, with all schools required to report results to their LEAs on optically marked record forms. LEAs were required to process these results and send to schools both a summary of their own results and a report on those of the LEA as a whole. All our headteachers sent their results to their LEA. The Innercity LEA sent back a ranked list of schools. The other three LEAs sent back to all their schools reports which gave an overall picture of all local Key Stage 1 results and their own results in a form that allowed ready comparisons with the average for the LEA, although not with other schools.

Of the 30 headteachers who answered our questionnaire in late 1991, 19 had presented their SAT results to governors. But only 11 of these had given a full explanation, usually as part of the head-teachers's termly report. The other eight had either 'mentioned' [them] 'talked informally' about them, or given a brief 'résumé' to the whole governing body or to one or two interested governors. In 1992, with more formal requirements in place, there was more communication with governors. Only two headteachers acknowledged that they did not present their results to governors; two others were unwilling to comment. The remaining 26 headteachers reported results to governors in some form or other and in varying degrees of detail; of these only 11 said they had had some feedback. This bore no relationship to the number of documents the headteacher had presented. Nine of these 11 reported that the governors were 'pleased' or 'very satisfied' and the other two reported that the presentations provoked discussion of such things as how the head-teacher felt about the results and how the results were being used to make changes. One of these two reported with some annoyance that governors were putting pressure on her:

So we have to be below county average in level 1s and above it in level 3s!

In summary, our information suggests that in 1992 heads were generally willing to inform governors. Governors, on the other hand, do not appear to have shown much interest.

As with governors, some schools were reluctant to communicate the results to parents. Altogether in 1991, 21 of the 26 class teachers informed parents of their child's individual results. Ten of the 21 gave results only to the parents who came to the school's open evening. Some teachers felt that parents would not understand the results unless they were given with an explanation:

If the parents had been confronted with the actual form (with numbers), they wouldn't have understood it without some kind of discussion with the teacher.

These findings correspond quite closely to those reported by Hughes *et al.* (1991).

The majority of headteachers (17) reported that parents were pleased with the information they received about their children's results: there were no further reactions. Two of these headteachers put this down to the hard work they themselves had done with parents. Responses from Y2 teachers in 1991 were very much in line with those of their heads, in particular that there was little feedback from parents:

> There was no feedback from parents after the results went out. I think they know us at this school and trust us to get on with it. They didn't show any particular interest in the levels, they seem to be mainly interested in our comments.

In 1992 the situation was more formal, with schools required, by law, to report to parents both the results of their own children and a summary of the school's overall results. All 30 headteachers remaining in our study did appear to meet the legal requirements, using either an LEA printout 'customized' to show individual results, or two separate sheets (individual results and LEA printout). One headteacher added a special explanatory letter to the report, and another offered explanatory notes and added a new section to the school end-of-year RoA portfolio.

Not surprisingly, more parental interest was reported than in the previous year. About half the headteachers reported some feedback or interest. However, 12 of the 30 headteachers said that they had had no feedback whatsoever: parents did not really want to know the levels. The remaining three headteachers reported only scant interest; one of them remarked that amidst the general apathy at his school, only the Bangladeshi parents were interested because testing was part of their culture, whereas it was not 'in most other systems'. The attitude towards parents differed between schools. Some appeared to let them in on the national assessment and enlist their help in various ways; some kept them in the dark, either because they claimed that they would not understand, or because they were scared of releasing parental pressure on themselves and their staff. Teachers were generally keen to stress that they themselves had not made the children aware of their levels, so that if children did know, it was not because the teachers had told them.

Some clearly felt that children might have become aware of their levels 'if parents mentioned levels after the report had been discussed'.

Guidance about publishing and reporting

Before the first reported run in 1992, not one of our LEAs gave schools any guidance about publishing, but implicitly sided with the 'anti-league table' view and did not actively encourage schools to publish results.

> We didn't give any guidance. If they wanted to publish, we wouldn't stop them . . . most of us are against that.

All four LEAs trod carefully, aware of the attitude of heads and teachers who had felt 'betrayed' after league tables were unexpectedly published in 1991.

In 1992, schools were required to report the results of national assessment to parents (their child's own individual scores and a comparative report across all Y2 children in the school). All four LEAs made an attempt to support schools with this and designed report forms and formats for schools to use if they so wished.

On the whole, the formats echoed the different LEA philosophies. Innercity left the decisions to headteachers and charged them for the service to get them used to local management of schools (LMS). Midboro did not want 'anything to be a surprise for teachers' and so provided everything and offered some choice while at the same time persuading schools to include other issues beyond levels and ATs. Northshire, assuming consensus, offered no choice and stressed national curriculum attainment and pupil targets. Homeshire could see that the way it had introduced the record was not conducive to it being well received, but felt powerless to do anything about it. All four LEAs, then, offered a framework for reporting to parents which aligned with their own particular philosophies, and overall, headteachers were pleased to have a format to follow which meant they did not have to do the work themselves.

LEA use of results

Initially, all our LEA contacts could see possible uses of results at local level – for example, in reviewing resource allocation, informing INSET requirements, and assisting inspectors in monitoring schools. After the first run of SATs in 1991, the LEAs (although not Innercity) did little more than produce two tables of results: an individual school printout and a general overview showing the percentage of children at each level on each AT. These they sent into schools, with no specific advice on how to use them.

Between 1991 and 1992, sceptical of the reliability of the results (and hence of their different positions on the government league table) all but Homeshire developed their own Optical Mark Reader sheets which recorded quite extensive contextual variables, including, for example, date of birth and provision of free school meals. The sheets were analysed in depth and the findings were disseminated to different audiences: headteachers, advisers, education committee and the DfE.

Midboro, Northshire and Innercity presented the 1992 findings to headteachers and impressed upon them that they should be comparing their results with local averages or with those of similar schools. There was more pressure on headteachers to discuss results with advisers in relation to school development plans. Midboro's analysis highlighted socio-economic factors which affect performance. Northshire's Education Committee was considering using the LEA's analysis of results to make changes to the county admission procedures. Based on an analysis of its 1992 results, Innercity was awarded a substantial grant to improve pupils' fluency in English.

Overall, three of our LEAs did more in-depth analysis after the 1992 assessment and fulfilled some of their original intentions. All three put increasing pressure on schools to use their results to improve the education on offer and two of them took their analysis further to try to effect changes in local procedures.

Conclusion

Despite heads' and teachers' early fears, in the event there were very few signs of pressure as a result of national assessment. In 1991 perhaps this was not surprising, given that schools were not required by law to communicate their results to any other agency, although heavy pressure was put on them to send them to their LEA. In these circumstances, schools behaved differently: those most ideologically opposed to the introduction of national assessment refused to inform anyone at all; others did not volunteer the results, but produced them when asked; many accepted that they should be routinely reported to LEAs, governors and parents. In no case was much feedback experienced, and only one or two instances of pressure were encountered. This was perhaps because of the fact that there was no base-line allowing easy comparison, or because of the general reticence of 'outsiders' in challenging professionals in the context of a new system that few were confident they understood. In the following year, 1992, once the pilot stage was over, full reporting was a legal requirement, although there were no nationally produced league tables of individual schools; as in 1991, league tables were published of LEAs. More information to enable comparisons was provided to parents and governors – for example, the LEA overall distributions. Nevertheless, there were still very few instances reported of feedback to schools or pressure on headteachers.

It would have been interesting to see whether there would have been growing awareness among parents, governors and LEAs, and more corresponding flexing of muscles, the following year. However, the union boycott in 1993 meant that momentum was lost and forced concessions by the government, including the agreement that there would be no requirement for publication of league tables at Key Stage 1.

Use of results in schools

The absence of the expected external pressure enabled headteachers to relax a little and to start to appreciate that the results of national assessment could be of positive benefit, internally, to themselves and to their teachers. This realization and its effect form the focus of this section. We should point out, however, that it is not always possible to distinguish the impact of results themselves from that of the experience of doing the assessment.

When heads and teachers were asked about their expectations regarding the use of results of national assessment, there was hardly any specific mention of the use of results within schools. Although national assessment and its results were intended to contribute to the improvement of education, respondents in early 1991 were vague as to how results would be used:

... teachers moderating their own expectations about children.

The uses of assessment may cause teachers to reflect on their methods and on their ability to make and keep records.

[Results] will enable teachers to look at what children in the schools have achieved.

Another teacher, reflecting on the situation in her own school, felt that headteachers might use the results 'to move resisters'. A few respondents thought results might contribute to better education for children if they 'pinpoint things children need help with and where to go'.

The main use of results in schools was expected to be the passing of results from one teacher to another so that 'the next teacher will have a better starting point', something which was found with the use of standardized test results in the early 1980s (Gipps *et al.* 1983). Transfer to junior, middle or secondary school was mentioned by several respondents, who felt that 'continuity' could result 'if records are read and properly used'.

Only two headteachers reported that they did not discuss the outcomes of the SATs in 1991 with their staff; the majority of headteachers organized whole-staff discussion.

In the six case-study schools the uses of results were discussed in interviews; 25 other schools returned questionnaires, in which descriptions of uses were often brief. Following the speculations about the non-usefulness of results during our early 1991 visits, we asked specifically, a year later, whether headteachers would use results as a basis for organizational change: 21 out of 31 said they would, the other ten saying that they would not. In addition, we asked an open-ended question about the uses envisaged for or made of the results. Six headteachers felt that the results were not significant enough to use in any way, one being content to leave them 'available for reference'. Twenty-four headteachers were using school results at three levels of intervention:

- pointing them at teachers to inform teaching and learning;
- consulting them to guide resourcing and budgeting;
- employing them as an indicator of school effectiveness.

However, it should also be said that many of the changes described were not in fact uses of the results themselves but the outcome of the experience of doing SATs. Some headteachers who were reviewing the curriculum stressed that this was not due solely to the results:

> We are always trying to improve our teaching, not just because of SATs.

Use and non-use of results

We analysed separately why some schools and teachers made no use of the results of the assessment programme, since this seems as important as any use that is made.

Headteachers

In 1991 ten headteachers claimed that they were not using the results as a basis for change. Straightforward denials and comments such as 'we are not changing our assessment practice' were common, although one headteacher qualified this with:

> not the results, no, but the reality of in-school testing has sharpened our view of assessment.

Some headteachers apparently resisted implementing change on the basis of a system they did not agree with:

> No, other than where it would match the decisions we had already [made], or would make as a result of the philosophy, practice, policy and belief we as a staff and school adhere to.

One headteacher elaborated along these lines his reasons for not using the 1991 results as a basis for change:

> We will continue with TA as usual and no policy decisions on SATs will be made until the SATs themselves are finally presented in a more permanent framework. Teachers are coping well enough. [These are] 'changes of the moment' and we must learn to separate the educational policies from the political policies.

By 1992 more headteachers (17) felt strongly that SATs were not worth doing. Reasons they gave for this were:

- 'SATs don't tell us anything we didn't know already.'
- The tasks are 'narrow' and do not represent good practice.

- The rewards are too small.
- 'I begrudge the time and the stress for teachers.'
- 'You won't get out as much as you put in.'
- Time spent on SATs delays curriculum development.
- SATs represent formal testing at age 7, which some headteachers strongly oppose.
- SATs are unfair and label certain children (especially bilingual learners).
- SAT results are unreliable because of the different ways teachers adapt the instructions and present the tasks.
- SATs represent a threat to teachers' investment in their work.

Teachers

We were able to analyse teachers' patterns of use and non-use in some detail. It is particularly interesting to look at this in relation to our models, described in Chapter 2. In 1993 our evidence gatherers looked at the national assessment records mainly to check what had been taught 'to see what a child had covered in Y1' and to make sure they, as teachers, 'didn't repeat topics'. At one school, for example, the teacher looked at the pupils' folders for evidence of which of the agreed 'two ATs per half term' had been covered and then planned what she would teach so that there would be 'no overlap'. This 'checking for coverage' seems to serve as the main use of records because these teachers admit to reassessing children on entry to their class. At a second school, the teacher was willing to accept previous science results, but she would repeat work and reassess children in both maths and English. The teacher in a third school said she would want to 'do revision' of the topics covered by the last teacher because 'children do forget'. Similarly, a fresh assessment was done for each child by the teacher in the first school, who kept her own 'AT book' using an elaborate triangle system (marking one side for 'experiencing', two sides for 'understanding' and three sides for 'achieved'). This has nothing to do with SoAs, and suggests that the teacher was not using them to plan progressively, as is the case with systematic planners.

Our systematic planners told us they were making more conscious use of results passed up. They were consulting them to see what level children had achieved in order to plan the next set of activities, and this helped them to put children into appropriate groups. One systematic integrator had made herself a grid for each AT, listing all the children's names and the levels they came up with when they joined her class. These teachers initially trusted the judgements made by the previous class teachers and did not consciously reassess the children when they came into their classes. But one teacher pointed out that the levels and passed-up 'can do' lists were not enough and that colleagues' subjective comments about children were also important.

In three schools, all containing intuitives, it became clear that the results were not seriously being consulted. Teachers attached more importance to their colleagues' comments about children than to recorded national curriculum results. Teachers at one very small school said:

> in a school this size, records are not so important because we are talking together about children all the time.

At another of these schools the teacher's strongly held philosophy stopped her from keeping any serious records before children even reached Y2:

> I wouldn't do any serious assessment of Y1 because they don't mature, their ideas don't come together until after the February half term in Y2, then they fly through it.

Overall, only the systematic planners can be said to have been using results in a way that shows trust in the judgement of colleagues and leads to progressive planning in relation to national curriculum levels. The evidence gatherers were really checking for evidence that ATs had been taught, but were compelled to check children's performance for themselves before moving children on. The intuitives were relying on the subjective comments and intuitive understandings of themselves and others, and records and other ways of providing evidence were seen as no more than a laborious chore.

Use of results by Year 3 teachers

One of the aims of the research was to evaluate the use of the assessment results by receiving teachers, as well as by the children's current teachers, and by those outside the school. To do this we sent questionnaires to Y3 teachers in our sample in the early autumn of both 1991 and 1992. (Where our study school was an infant school,

Table 6   Uses made by Y3 teachers of results passed up to them 1991
(N = 36)

Using assessment information to form groups	20
Using assessment information for curriculum planning	25
Using assessment information for individual work programmes	23

we sent the questionnaires to the relevant junior school.) In 1991 we received replies from 36 Y3 teachers (in 28 schools) and in 1992 25 replies (from 23 schools).

On both questionnaires we attempted to determine what use Y3 teachers made of the results that were passed up to them. In the earlier questionnaire we offered three suggestions for teachers to tick, in addition to an 'Other' category. Results are shown in Table 6. In most cases teachers ticked more than one of these uses, and in ten cases they ticked all three. There were few explanations of these choices; five teachers explained how they used assessment information for individual work programmes, mainly to identify children with special needs. Two teachers said they would use information to form groups for maths. Only two teachers said they did not use assessment information at all.

Overall, only seven Y3 teachers in the 1991 questionnaire found results useful:

> Since national assessment arrangements I am more aware of how children learn in stages and steps. You can pinpoint what's wrong easier. SoAs are real guidance.

In the 1992 questionnaire we addressed the question of use of results in a different way, hoping to elicit a more specific and meaningful response. We asked: 'Have you used these levels to inform your planning for this school year?' We asked for explanation of either a 'yes' or 'no' reply. With this more open-ended questioning, replies varied (see Table 7). Devising and planning individual work programmes, sometimes called differentiation, was the main use claimed by teachers, although this was rarely explained except in very general terms such as 'making sure that the work offered to each child is suitable for their ability'.

A few teachers also used results for 'informing planning and ensuring a range of ability in social groupings'. However, grouping

Table 7   Use by Y3 teachers of assessment levels 1992 (*N* = 25)

For groupwork/forming groups	5
For devising individual work programmes/differentiation	10
To plan topic work	4
As information/'starting point'	5

children according to their assessment results and using results as a 'starting point' were controversial points that some teachers felt strongly about.

On the positive side, one teacher felt that the results:

> make forward planning much more realistic [because] you do not want to wait for a term to gauge children's ability. You are aware of where to start with children and have realistic aims of what they can achieve.

On the other hand, some teachers who claimed to find the results useful nevertheless made it clear they wanted to make a fresh start every year: they did not want their knowledge of the results to cloud their judgement of the children coming up to them. Some felt it was 'not right to look at the documents' before they knew the children, as this might prejudice their ideas towards the child at the beginning of term:

> I work on the basis of trying to estimate ability levels by working with the children rather than looking at records initially.

> Assessment results from the previous years are used after half term to inform actual decisions made by the new class teacher.

Some teachers implied that the information supplied by the Y2 teachers was both more useful and more trustworthy than results of testing. Six Y3 teachers from 1991 insisted that the Y2 teacher's comments gave them more useful information than national assessment results:

> I have a good working relationship with my Y2 colleague and I find consulting and discussing with her more valuable.

> I still feel visiting the children in Y2 and looking at their work, talking to them and to their teacher is more useful.

The following comments from 1991 demonstrate how four Y3 teachers wanted more than objective results; they wanted subjective information about children:

> We value teachers' comments on children's character, not just attainment.

> I spoke to the other teacher about grouping . . . I didn't use records for that.

> When you receive any new class you spend a few weeks getting to know them and their ability. Anyone not straightforward and you ask the previous teacher . . . share feelings and consult records and reports.

> Assessment is a priority in filling forms but in teaching terms you need to look at the whole child, Personal and Social Education (PSE), etc. as part of the assessment.

One teacher felt that such information could best be obtained from the child:

> You find out about special needs children anyway from talking to the child. You can spot special needs children from looking at pieces of work the teacher sends up to you.

Results as a reflection of children's true attainment

In the 1992 questionnaire we asked whether teachers thought that the results reflected children's true attainment, as in the previous questionnaire in 1991 some teachers indicated that national assessment levels were too broad to indicate true attainment:

> There is too wide a band between levels, the information is not a true reflection of a child's ability. Our own tests, assessments and teacher-based observations are much more use.

Another junior school teacher felt that the children who were put at level 3 by the Y2 teacher *were* generally level 3 in her own experience, whereas the levels of other children were less reliable:

> The numbers used in standardized tests are useful. National assessment is just too broad. Level 3 proved to be more reliable than the other levels.

One junior school had also applied its own assessment of children in Y3, but in contrast to the above, found a match, for the majority of children, with the results identified by the Y2 teachers.

In the second questionnaire about half of the teachers (13) felt that levels were a true picture of attainment, giving a 'fair overview' on the whole. Three teachers felt that the true attainment was reflected in the child's present work in Y3 because the children were 'working at the next level with confidence'. The team teachers, however, noted that some children may just have achieved a level and may need consolidation work at that level.

Three Y3 teachers assumed a true reflection of attainment because they trusted the testing process which had resulted in the levels:

They have been rigorously applied and moderated.

The children are monitored as they are being tested. Tests are all the same for each child.

They do give an indication of the child's level but levels are so vast that you often have to go back over the levels.

Another teacher was more specifically critical:

There has to be some question of the validity of science.

Some teachers indicated that the results reflected children's attainment as being higher than it seemed in Y3:

Some of the SATs partially reflect children's ability. Some were easier than others, so don't truly reflect the level of attainment.

Conversely, some indicated that children had been underestimated in their results from Y2:

[Results] give a fair overview of attainment, however, some children did not perform to their true ability through nerves.

Six Y3 teachers were not sure whether results were a true picture of attainment or not, citing some of the criticisms noted about testing format and children's varying levels of retention for their uncertainty.

Response of Year 3 teachers

In 1992, children could be assessed at level 4 for the first time. National results (DfE 1992) indicate that small numbers of children

Table 8 Range of levels in results passed up to Y3 teachers, 1992

W–1	1
W–3	9
W–4	4
1–3	6
1–4	2
2–3	1

achieved level 4, most notably in reading (2%) and data handling (5%).

Although some LEAs, some heads and some teachers had indicated to us that they definitely would not be testing children at level 4, it was clear that some children in our sample would achieve level 4. As this had clear implications for the Y3 teacher receiving the children, we asked Y3 teachers to indicate the range of levels represented in the results handed up to them from Y2. The results received by Y3 teachers show some surprising variations (Table 8). The majority of schools (17) used levels up to 3. Only six schools used the whole range of levels from W to 4, with two of these using 1–4. It is also surprising that one school used only W–1. The Y3 teacher receiving this cohort of children commented that she would:

> cater for it in my classroom – and appreciate that a '1' encompasses a wide range of ability.

Year 3 teachers were asked how they felt about this spread of results. Seventeen considered the spread 'fair', 'representative', 'normal' or 'as expected'. The remaining teachers commented on the spread of results according to how it would affect them as Y3 teachers. A few teachers found the prospect of dealing with such a wide range of levels worrying, or mentioned the extra work involved in planning for an extra level or dealing with different levels within a large class of 34 children.

One teacher who inherited a spread of levels from 1 to 4 claimed that the school's maths scheme catered for level 4 children and that 'we team-teach in order to cope with it'. Some teachers acknowledged the need to plan with the level 4 child in mind so that 'the work will be matched to the child's ability':

> A level 4 child is working within level 5 – the teacher needs to bear this in mind.

Extending at academic level without isolating the child. Range of extension/open-ended activities needs to be greater, with greater resourcing for levels 3/4.

Planning at appropriate level rather than 'assuming' at lower level and so repeating work. Awareness that they may 'just' be level 4 and need to consolidate this.

One Y3 teacher even saw advantages:

> The spread is consistent with Y4 children already in class. Therefore grouping is easier.

Junior schools do more standardized tests than infant schools and traditions of testing were well entrenched in the juniors. Many Y3 teachers were still partial to this kind of testing, and saw it as more valuable than national assessment. One Y3 teacher implied that Y2 teachers were now better able to judge children's attainment because 'they talk to children more than before to find out what they know'; but overall, Y3 teachers remained sceptical that results could provide more reliable information than they obtained previously from visits to Y2 classes, children's folders and standardized test scores. More importantly, they doubted the national assessment numbers. Eleven Y3 teachers doubted that the results reflected children's true level of attainment. Five teachers responded at a practical level, explaining that their experience of the children in Y3 did not match the results given to the same child in Y2. One teacher explained that while the results reflected attainment in most areas in 1992, they were less representative in the children's writing. Another teacher from 1991 was more specific:

> Some children were put as level 2 and we at the junior school would actually consider them special needs. That child was put down as level 2, average, and he is not average at all.

However, Y3 teachers did not want to attribute this mismatch of results to their Y2 colleagues' judgement about the children and they attributed various reasons for the mismatch between the level assigned to the child in Y2 and their own experiences of the child in Y3. The teacher quoted above attributed the mismatch to the advice from the moderator at the infants school to 'put children at level 2 when in doubt'. Others blamed children's lack of retention for the difference between the Y2 teacher's assessment of the child and their own. Four Y3 teachers felt that children may have achieved a level in Y2 which they did not now retain in Y3.

You have to take into account the long summer holiday break ... some children regress.

They seem to have forgotten what they've supposedly achieved.

Eight were critical of assessment itself, or what one teacher called 'the inaccuracy of the testing format and type'. Some specifically blamed SATs as a 'testing situation' which results in children who 'react in different ways on different days to different situations'. Others criticized the spread within one level and 'the enormous difference between a *just* level 2 and a *nearly* level 3'.

In summary, our data show that most Y3 teachers received detailed national assessment information for the children who came up to them from Y2 in both 1991 and 1992. While some teachers found this information 'nothing new', others, especially junior school teachers, as opposed to those in all-through primaries or first schools, welcomed the more 'precise' information given by results. Year 3 teachers generally did not find national assessment results useful in 1991, although this had changed by 1992 when they were becoming more familiar with national assessment and more aware of the levels. Some Y3 teachers did not agree with the levels that had been assigned to children in Y2, however, they did not blame Y2 teachers for this mismatch, but instead attributed it to the tests themselves, to the long summer break, or to children's variations in performance on different days.

The early years: conclusion

Initial concerns about the use of results were in the event not borne out by the 1991 and 1992 testing programmes. Certainly, headteachers felt betrayed by the government in the publication of the LEA league tables in 1991, which was supposed to be a pilot year. By late 1992, possibly in an attempt to deflect the teacher boycott of the 1993 assessment programme, the DfE announced that results of seven- and 14-year-olds would not be published as school league tables. This decision lifted the pressure on teachers to some extent, but by 1993 parents knew about national curriculum levels and heads knew that school-level results would be available in one form or another. Would the pattern of reacting to results, and making some changes to teaching and curriculum, alter?

What happened in 1993?

In 1993 fifteen headteachers received results from the Y2 teachers. Because of the unions' instructions, teachers were not obliged to present results to their heads and hence four of our headteachers did not 'officially' see the SAT results, although in reality they did look at them. As one headteacher put it: 'I looked, but didn't touch – silly, isn't it?' Clearly, union advice was taken but seen as something of a charade by some. Only four of these headteachers sent the information to the LEA. One sent all the actual booklets that the children had completed and another sent all the scores, thinking to himself. 'Why put yourself over a barrel?' Our other schools (across all four LEAs) refused to send the results to the LEA. When we talked to the LEA contacts, they reported the following returns: Midboro had four schools return results; Innercity had one; Homeshire had 50%; and Northshire had 12%. Four schools did not report results to parents/governors and there were mixed reactions to this. In the school that did not do SATs at all, the parents did not mind: they were offered a meeting but declined. In another two schools the parents did not say anything. As one headteacher put it:

> No one asked anything – even though for the last two years they have had the numbers – there was not one query when no numbers appeared.

The other 15 schools (including those in which the headteachers 'had not seen' them) gave parents some kind of feedback on their children's results. These were reported in a variety of ways: one or two *did* give the 'aggregated level', but most of the others gave 'TA levels only', 'results in broad terms', 'subject levels only', 'no levels, just narrative' and in one case, as lip-service to union action, parents 'got TA levels actually SAT results but called TA'. Mostly results were on an individual level and not comparative. Two headteachers in Homeshire published their results in their brochures. The results had not been validated by the LEA and other headteachers were 'alarmed' at their action.

Parents' reactions to the results varied. Eight headteachers reported that they had had no reaction ('not a mention') from the parents while seven reported that the parents were pleased and supportive. Of those that gave results in terms of aggregated levels, there was a feeling that parents did not really understand what they were reading.

Headteachers' reactions to the test results were mixed. Two made no comment while nine were happy with the results, especially if they were an improvement on the previous year, and one volunteered 'they were up, have been consistently up over the last three years'. Two were disappointed and thought the results should have been higher – one thought this was because the children did not understand the formats and another put it down to having changed the school maths and science schemes only recently. Four years into our study in the third round of SATs, there were now only four headteachers who maintained that SATs simply confirmed what teachers already knew about children's attainment. Another headteacher, whom we had placed in the intuitive group, complained every year that there was something fundamentally wrong with the SATs because children kept scoring higher in the science tests than on TA. Again, in 1993 the children had scored higher and the head argued:

> There's either something wrong with those SATs or there's something wrong with my Y2 teacher – my money is on my Y2 teacher. I can't believe she doesn't know her children.

7

THE IMPACT OF
NATIONAL ASSESSMENT

Introduction

As we pointed out in Chapter 1, the government's intention was that educational standards would be raised as an outcome of the national curriculum and its related assessment procedures. In late 1992 we asked headteachers whether they were seeing any evidence of this. In answer to our question, three headteachers were not willing to commit themselves. The majority, however, felt that the quality of education *was* improving.

Seventeen of the 27 headteachers who responded were of the opinion that the introduction of national assessment was a good thing and was improving the quality of education. Testing alone had not been of particular value, but education in general was improving because doing TA as part of an objectives model had focused teachers' attention on their own practice. In particular:

- by looking at SoAs for TA, teachers had improved their understanding of what an individual child could actually do;
- by having the curriculum listed in SoAs as a series of objectives,

teachers could ensure the child made progress and this could raise their expectations particularly of the most able;
- the spelling out of objectives (in maths in particular) had improved teaching of the basics;
- the process of moderation had forced teachers to interact, negotiate meanings for SoAs and, hence, standardize judgements made about individual children and 'levelness';
- mandatory assessment had made some teachers look back to their planning and evaluate what they do.

These positive headteachers still had some reservations, however: any improvement was at the cost of overload for teachers generated by extra paperwork and 'some trauma' in coping with change.

In autumn 1993 we again put a direct question to headteachers about the further impact of the national curriculum assessment on schools. Despite the perceived pressure, eight of the nineteen who responded again felt that national assessment had generally 'made teaching better'. It had 'made teaching more focused' and 'made practice far more rigorous'. Teachers were 'certainly a lot more critical of their work' and 'had learned a lot from going through the process'.

The headteachers had noticed changes in teachers' thinking which they felt was for the better. For example, national curriculum levels had given teachers 'a sense of basic benchmarks which had affected their thinking' and in some cases had shown teachers 'that their expectations should be higher'. There was a better understanding of group work, teachers were 'designing tasks more successfully' and there was 'more differentiation' of the curriculum to meet individual needs.

In 1992 ten headteachers clearly felt that national assessment *was not* improving the quality of education. The arguments proposed were as follows:

- As a procedure, national assessment is independent of the quality of teaching. The quality of education received, however, is not.
- Because the model included SATs, it was narrowing the curriculum by encouraging teachers to teach to the test.
- Assessment may have helped teachers to evaluate what they delivered, and they could see where input was needed, but they were grossly under-funded in most cases and this led to personal stress because they were unable to meet their own objectives.

Hence the quality of education was not improving due to teacher frustration over lack of resources.

Given the national furore over Key Stage 1 testing, that many of the headteachers could see improvement in the planning, teaching and assessment process seemed surprising. It is important, however, to note that this was by no means a simple result of imposing tests and teaching towards them. It is a more complex process involving teachers' assessment, planning and teaching skills. This improvement in their skills was partly based on close observation of children's performance in relation to assessment criteria (a skill developed through doing the early SATs), and partly from a variety of activities, including discussion with other teachers about what SoAs meant, in order to arrive at TA judgements, independent of SAT results. If, at Key Stage 2, the SATs are standardized paper and pencil tests with TA only required after the tests are done and against very broad-level descriptions without any form of moderation, then there may not be the same impact on practice at this stage as there had been at Key Stage 1.

We now look at the impact on various aspects of teaching and assessment practice.

Impact on curriculum and teaching

Headteachers' early views

Nationally, maths results in 1991 and 1992 were lower than those for English and science. This may have been an artefact of the curriculum or the tests rather than due to any shortcomings in the teaching. Nevertheless, the consequence was that in 1991 the main area for development was seen to be maths:

> We felt that maths – looking at [the results] alongside the others – was an area that needed a bit of development. Possibly we need to do a bit more in reception.

Twelve headteachers used results to focus on maths. Five of these commented on the new emphasis on instant recall:

> We felt there were elements of maths that needed sharpening up, such as mental response in arithmetic ... We've

encouraged, right through the school, not to go back to chanting tables, but to insist on a response from the children over mental arithmetic.

Two headteachers mentioned number bonds:

> We haven't made our children learn number bonds to 20 plus or minus, by rote before! Five seconds to find the pineapple . . .

Two volunteered that they may have previously 'concentrated on the outcomes rather than the processes' in maths. One proposed the need to focus on particular mathematical vocabulary, while another felt that changes needed to be made in the teaching of subtraction and division:

> The subtraction showed us that we are still influenced by our own experience, that subtraction and division are harder than adding and multiplication. We are trying to teach them now as more simultaneous procedures to avoid that inference continuing.

One of the areas of change mentioned or implied by four headteachers was teaching style. Two saw the SATs tasks, in particular the 1991 practical maths and science tasks, as providing new things for teachers to do:

> Some of the tasks proved so successful with the children that there has been an influence on the teaching style and approaches found within the class.

> Certainly we are using the process [of national assessment] as a way in to teach all staff about observation of children's learning.

Two headteachers commented on the change to a more formal teaching style:

> Work is beginning to be more formal, which is not a bad thing. [There are] spelling tests, tables, mental arithmetic, which are going to involve a greater formality in the classroom.

Another, however, did not see the change to a more formal style as a good thing:

> I really think [SATs] will ultimately change the way teachers
> are teaching because the government [is] determined that they
> will. I don't think that's good.

After the 1992 assessment, only ten headteachers said they were
making no changes to the curriculum as a result of Key Stage 1
assessment. The other 21 appeared to be rethinking priorities in
relation to what was to be taught in some or all of the core subjects.
Again, maths was the most widely mentioned subject: 15 headteachers reported that the maths results had prompted some kind
of review and/or action. Of these, five mentioned changing to
a new school maths scheme to fit more closely with national
curriculum targets. Four mentioned that the results had identified
'shortfall areas' in their curriculum coverage (but did not specify
which). However, another four did specify where more work was
needed and what they decided to do, namely, 'develop mental
maths', 'more number bond drilling', 'more use of calculators', 'the
application of algorithms'. One of these 15 headteachers focused
on teaching and had encouraged 'more practical sessions' through
extra staff provision. The remaining headteacher had given more
attention to the reception and Y1 children and was reviewing the
content of the maths curriculum at this stage.

Six of the headteachers mentioned above also described changes
made to the English curriculum. Although one loosely described
these changes as merely giving 'different emphasis' to the profile
components, the others were more specific, mentioning writing,
handwriting and reading. Four headteachers reported attention to
writing: two said they were paying more attention to the 'structure',
'mechanics' and 'basics' of writing, one had decided to 'start
independent writing earlier' and the other to teach joined-up
handwriting earlier. One headteacher was focusing on 'clear targets
for reading with quantifiable aims in mind'. Only one said there
would be changes made to the science curriculum, which indicated
a move away from integrating science into the general classroom
topic: her teachers were to 'undertake science in a positive manner,
if necessary as separate topics'. This headteacher also intended
making changes in maths.

Six headteachers said they were reviewing all the core subjects,
and not just in Y2. Three of these felt a need to focus on the content
of the core curriculum being delivered at reception and Y1 level

(one looking particularly at general issues). Two intended to adapt what was being taught in order to 'match the SATs' more closely. The remaining headteacher gave us her list of intentions which reflected concerns reported by many of our other respondents:

1 Spend more time in nursery on language development.
2 Extend work for more able children, with a view to levels 3 and 4.
3 Target English as an area for development.
4 Teach capitals, full stops, development of stories.
5 Decide *not* to teach joined-up writing – job for junior school.
6 Spend five to 10 minutes per day on mental arithmetic.
7 Consider whether we are underestimating in TA: look at teacher expectation, gender and differentiation.

Interestingly, one area which seems to be coming under review is the early years' curriculum (reception and Y1), although the headteacher quoted above was the only one to mention the nursery curriculum.

Teachers' early views

As well as asking heads about changes, we wanted to find out what the teachers did as a result of testing. In late 1991 we asked the Y2 teachers whether they had made any changes since doing SATs in 1991 and we offered them three areas for consideration: curriculum content, methods of teaching, and grouping of children. While many teachers had made changes in one or more of these areas, some had strong feelings that they did not want to be influenced by the SATs or their results. One teacher commented that she would 'change in response to the ATs, not to the SATs'.

Following the 1991 results, a few teachers identified areas to focus on in their teaching. Eleven out of 26 teachers said they had made changes in curriculum content following the 1991 SATs, although again it is difficult to determine to what extent this is due to the results rather than the SAT experience. At least four of these 11 were concentrating on maths, as maths scores had been lower than the other subjects:

> SATs [results] have highlighted maths as an area for concern this year . . . the children should have done better.

We felt that our children achieved poorly on a number of facts and patterns [in maths]. So we're trying to focus when they are younger, earlier on in the year. Trying to do a bit more mental arithmetic, just at the odd moment.

Some teachers were using their 1991 experience of assessment as a guideline for assessing children in the future. This meant that they were using the SAT materials, or adapting some of the SATs methods, as part of their teaching style.

Six teachers out of 26 said they had made changes in their method of teaching following SATs, although comments throughout the questionnaire indicate that more than this have probably made such changes. One teacher was aware of changes in her teaching style:

I have become more formal in the way I teach spelling. I've actually started giving my two able groups in language spellings to learn at home and spelling tests when those words are done.

Three teachers commented on the way they now asked children to work more independently, so that they could concentrate on working with groups of children:

During the SATs you had to have the discipline to sit with the group and concentrate your whole effort on that group. It taught me how to do it. Before the SATs I couldn't do that.

I've always concentrated on one group at a time, having introduced the session to the whole group. Since SATs, I'm more aware of the need for concentrated sessions. Occasionally I say I want *no* interruptions at all.

We also noted changes in approaches to TA. Half of the respondents said that doing the 1991 SATs affected the way they were approaching their TA in 1992.

We have changed our reading assessment along the lines of the SAT.

The activities used in the SATs have given me ideas for some classroom teaching and TA.

Speaking and listening – I'm giving more opportunities, in things like the home corner, not just play.

It gave me more ideas for TA – how to make them less of a 'test' especially maths.

In addition, there was some indication that teachers were moving more towards 'teaching to the test' now that they had a better idea of what the test involved and what kind of results they could expect. In all, five out of 26 said they had made changes in order to give children a fairer chance on the SATs:

I will give the children activities that will prepare them for SATs (e.g. storywriting with spelling help).

'Teaching towards it'.

I'm concentrating a lot more on Ma3 [learning number facts] because I know that one's going to be tested.

I might be tempted to push for accuracy of punctuation earlier than I would normally, although this could be to the detriment of the child's long-term development of style and creativity.

I'm starting to do mental arithmetic.

Teachers who had done SATs in 1991 reported changes in their awareness, knowledge and confidence in national assessment generally. Many of the changes highlight an increased awareness of individual children's achievements and possibilities for intervention by teachers. Some teachers were reluctant to accept SAT results. Because they felt that they had both a knowledge of children and understanding of what was required for each level of attainment, they could be critical of the SAT where it did not match their own assessment. But 22 out of 26 said that the SAT had helped them to get a feel for the national curriculum levels:

Yes, I do have a feel for the levels now. When you hear children reading, you see them at a level.

It made me much more aware of the standards which I should expect for each level.

Maths was the hardest to get to grips with in the beginning, so I suppose I must have worked harder on the maths. The science . . . and the English [I found] much quicker to become familiar [with].

The experience of SATs also helped teachers to feel happier and more familiar with the statements of attainment. Twenty-three teachers said the SoAs were clearer to them than before SATs, and 24 said they were more familiar with them:

> Yes, I'm more familiar with the SoAs now, more aware of them. I have an awareness now of what they are overall. I have them in mind and I have some idea of what activities might match up.

> Especially with the language. I can say 'oh, yes, level 2, level 3'. They are certainly starting to be 'just there' in my head.

One teacher demonstrated the thoroughness of her familiarity by giving the example of Ma3 level 2:

> They actually need to know their number bonds. And it actually means *know* in terms of mental arithmetic. This is different from 'can work out' (level 1) using support material.

The teacher went on to describe the usefulness of this familiarity with SoAs in explaining to parents what 'know' really means:

> Can they say '7 + 2 = 9', just like that? If they're throwing two dice at home, rather than working it out, can they just jump up and give the answer? That's the difference between the levels.

A few teachers explained how they incorporated their new-found familiarity with levels and SoAs into their teaching practice:

> Constantly, in your mind, you're keeping level 2 because you know the children should be reaching level 2.

> I'm still teaching the activities at level 2, even if they got level 2, because I can see what we're working towards to get level 3. I group my children according to maths ability so that I know when I take a group that I'm 'teaching to level 1' or 'to level 2'. So being confident and knowing all about levels certainly helps teaching.

> In terms of language, you've got some who are still just writing strings of letters. You know they're not going to reach level 2. Just have to work at their level, pushing them to level 1.

Longer-term changes in teaching

By 1993 only 11 of the original 32 Y2 teachers with whom we
started working in 1991 remained as Y2 teachers in the same
school. When reflecting over the period between the 1992 and
1993 SATs, ten of the 11 teachers said they had made changes in
the teaching of maths. The main thrust had been aimed at giving
children practice in instant recall, or 'mental maths':

> Based on last year's results, the Y2 staff have been asked to
> take any opportunity to practice mental maths and to do it
> every day.

> We do ten minutes a day and this has paid off.

Four teachers, all judged to be systematic planners (see Chapter
2) reported changes in the teaching of spelling. Three of the schools
have bought in spelling schemes. One school allotted specific time
to the teaching of spelling, not integrating it into topic work, and
was setting children for spelling. The second school made changes
in teaching and testing 'definitely because of SATs; otherwise we
wouldn't have bothered'. The children learned some words every
week at home and the teacher 'will do a little test while hearing
reading'. This led to arranging children in different groups. The
teacher at the third school 'has changed her spelling tactics'. She
sends home 20 spellings to be learned every weekend. Then she
does 'not a test' but 'a relaxed quiz with lots of success'. One
teacher, judged to be intuitive, has had 'just a look at materials'
(of which she was highly critical) and 'begun to talk about it'.

After the 1992 SATs, joined-up handwriting seemed to have
been the main focus of attention over the year for another four of
our schools. Of these, only one seemed to have had no reservations
about teaching it much earlier than before (now in reception); the
others were less certain. Overall, six schools had changed their
ways of teaching handwriting, albeit with a degree of reluctance
from the teachers judged to be either evidence gatherers or
intuitives. The confident intuitive mentioned above had decided
that changing her tactics would be a waste of time because handwriting was:

> not an area worth bothering about – you get so little back.
> The children always score low.

Four teachers had made no changes to the way in which they were approaching writing. The other seven were adapting their teaching in some way, all mentioning more teaching of 'capitals and full stops', 'punctuation' and 'sentence structure'. As an example, one teacher described what she had been doing since the 1992 SATs:

> I've been putting up imperfect sentences on the blackboard and getting them to correct them. I've been getting in as much punctuation as I can at the same time. I haven't done that sort of thing for a long time.

Other changes that were mentioned were 'removing the reliance on word books and encouraging redrafting', 'encouraging more writing for audiences', 'more story-writing', 'more creative writing with bilingual children'. At only two schools did the teachers report introducing work on grammar into their teaching of English. Clearly, at one, the teacher had not previously thought of grammar as suitable for infants:

> Never before as an infant activity have we taught grammar.

Lists of verbs and nouns are produced for the children to use in sentence making. Similarly, at the other, children are taught about 'naming words' and 'doing words' as part of 'putting more stress on sentence structure'. Only two teachers mentioned reading. No details were given about changes in actual teaching, but 'reading books are being changed much more systematically' and children were being given more practice in reading aloud.

By 1993 changes were taking place in science teaching: four teachers had made some changes to science teaching over the year. The changes mentioned were 'devising new "can do" lists and trying to get children to say what they know', looking more closely at the criteria for AT1 and trying to bear them in mind when setting up tasks, 'consciously trying to get the children to pose more questions, particularly for AT1' and making science a discreet 'Monday afternoon activity' rather than integrating it into topic work 'because it was becoming very knowledge-based'.

Reasons given for the changes varied. Although the teachers in four schools were open in saying it was the SATs that had made them change, other teachers justified the changes they had made over the year by referring to the children's attitudes, needs and interests. At one school they had assigned 'magnets and shadows' to Y1 and 'electricity' to Y2. The teacher justified this by saying 'Y2 love circuits'.

Teaching to the test

In 1991 headteachers in four schools addressed the issue of 'teaching to the test' so that results, on paper at least, could be improved. One referred to 'working on strategies to help children cope with the tests'. Another, giving the example of practice drills in instant recall of number facts, said:

> People are more aware of what's called for. [We will be] teaching to it [the test] to some extent, to give the children a better chance.

A third, also referring to practice in instant recall, justified the need for this practice:

> Obviously, we must look to ensuring that the children have a fair amount of experience and practice in what's required. Otherwise, it would be very unfair for them to be faced with something they hadn't done before.

A fourth explained her reservations about 'teaching for the SAT':

> We are debating about brushing up on areas where there were a lot of level 1s. But this would be bolted on – and what basis for good practice is that?

By 1993 eight out of the 11 schools were beginning to reconsider *when* certain ATs would be taught – spreading the responsibility across the infant years and taking the pressure off the Y2 teachers at the end of the key stage. Some schools were much more specific about this than others, as in one case:

> More and more this year the infant department is carefully reconsidering when different ATs and levels will be taught, whether in reception, Y1 or Y2. We call this 'year-by-year objectives'.

Similarly, the teaching times of some topics, particularly in English and science, had been thought through (Table 9). The two schools not mentioned in Table 9 were less specific, but implied some kind of timetabling. The evidence from school F leaves no doubt about the impact of assessment on curriculum organization.

Table 9   Changes in teaching in six schools, 1993

School	AT/topic	Formerly taught	Now taught
A	Magnets	Y2	Y1
	Shadows	Y2	Y1
	Joined-up handwriting	Y4	R–Y2
B	Capitals/full stops	Y2	Y1
C	Capitals/full stops	Y2	Y1
	Joined-up handwriting	Y3	To some Y2
D	Joined-up handwriting	Y2/Y3	Reception
E	Capitals/full stops	To Y2 children who were ready	To all Y2 children
	Sun/shadows	Summer term, Y2	Before SAT in Y2
F	Whatever is to be in SAT	Various	Before the SAT

It must be said, however, that not all the teachers were happy about these changes. At school B the teacher's choice of words and tone of voice implied that she did not approve:

> Everything is being taught earlier and earlier . . . this kind of thing used to be done in Y2.

It was 'very frustrating' for the teacher at school E to find she could not spend as long as she would wish on some topics because SATs were imminent.

> I would normally leave sun and shadows until the summer term, but now we have to do it for SATs, so I have to hurry up and do it.

The head of a newly amalgamated school was grateful that assessment had made teachers 'tighten up' but, unfortunately, it had at the same time 'exposed the weaknesses, and there are an awful lot of them'. Another reported that, although teaching had become more focused, teachers were now doing *less* teaching.

Three heads (who were happy with the existing ways of working in their schools) were adamant that the teachers had not changed their methods in any way. However, others reported that there seemed to be less of 'the relaxed approach' to teaching, less 'giving children time to be creative', and this had 'really got to those who like to teach children, not subjects'. In addition, some teachers were complaining 'I can't cover those targets in *topic* anymore' and their 'teaching was becoming much more subject-based'. A Midboro head (although of the opinion that general practice was more rigorous) bemoaned the fact that teachers are 'actually addressing target delivery more than programmes of study'. She observed teaching now to be 'deliver assess, deliver assess, deliver assess – which is all a bit mechanistic'. A Northshire adviser had noticed that 'the level of spontaneity in teaching has been reduced' and the Homeshire adviser felt strongly that national curriculum assessment had 'disintegrated teaching' because:

> teachers have to focus on individuals to get the assessments right – they simply have got to tick those boxes'.

Longer-term impact: the LEA view

By 1993 our LEA contacts felt that there had been a significant impact on schools leading to a shift in thinking, as the following quotation indicates:

> A strong, strong, impact. National assessment has caused a sea change in terms of the way primary schools are working with children and in the way statistics are viewed. There has been a shift in perceptions.
>
> (Inspector for assessment, Innercity)

We will look at the two strands of this sea change in turn.

As to changes in the way primary schools are working, three of our LEA assessment advisers were beginning to see a move towards assessment-led teaching. In Innercity:

> There has been a significant shift in thinking about the role of assessment in teaching and learning: teachers are much more purposeful about the knowledge they are imparting to children. In the borough we are beginning to see assessment-led teaching.

Similarly, in Homeshire our contact reported that assessment co-ordinators, who are often systematic planners:

tend to plan for assessment rather than planning a programme of study and assessing it. In some schools there is one
day a week for assessment, some teachers have an assessment
book: once a fortnight all the children do a piece of work in
this book.

Our evidence gatherers had also been observed in Homeshire and
the adviser commented that some of them were clearly focusing on
SoAs and that being 'quite clear about what it is they want to assess
makes evidence gathering easier'. A contact in Northshire reported
'a lot of attainment-target-led curricula in that first year' but seems
to think this has eased a little since. He did, however, report 'more
emphasis on things like punctuation' (which is, after all, one of the
key criteria in gaining level 2 in writing and, therefore, suggests
assessment-led teaching), but argued that there is 'very little practising for the tests themselves'. Our Midboro contact said that in the
early days some teachers, thinking that they were preparing for the
SATs, introduced mini-tests and the LEA 'had to discourage this'.
    In looking at the way statistics are viewed, the 'statistics' are
school results and the results will be 'viewed' by schools themselves
and 'viewed' by others who see them reported in national league
tables. This clearly makes heads and teachers extremely accountable. Northshire observes that since the early years of national
assessment, parents have put more pressure on teachers and that
teachers have become concerned about keeping evidence of attainment. This concern was echoed in Homeshire and our contact
reported that by making children do work in a fortnightly assessment book, some teachers had found 'a safe way of approaching
the issue of accountability, certainly in terms of [having] evidence'.
The Midboro adviser reports that although, in general, parents
trust the schools (as found in an LEA survey), headteachers will
become accountable to another pressure group when OFSTED
inspectors make their visits.
    Within this context of accountability, our LEA representatives
were able to report on how schools were reacting to their own
results. The Innercity schools 'are definitely using results and
identifying gaps', and in Midboro 'heads' attitudes to processed
information [results are] definitely changing' and they are using
them to look at school performance. Our Northshire adviser has
observed that 'heads are showing more leadership due to the legal

responsibilities of reporting' and this has led to 'more professional activities' going on in schools, such as interpretation of SoAs, agreement trialling, the development of record-keeping systems and whole-school planning:

> It has gone from individual planning in isolation by isolated teachers to collaboration and planning together. This makes a child's route through school much more fluent. Children are less likely to be repeating the same material.

This type of professional activity is also observed in Innercity, where:

> Heads are putting together policy on how to record assessment and how to report attainment – attention to assessment is appearing in SDPs [School Development Plans] and inspectors are aware of this.

In Northshire schools are reported to have made decisions to spread the national curriculum across all of the infant years (from reception to Y2) and assess as the children go. (We have evidence of this in NAPS data from schools in all four LEAs.) The underlying assumption seems to be that if schools decide when ATs should be taught and assessed, the chances are they will get more children to higher levels by the end of the key stage.

Overall, then, the LEA advisers felt that assessment has crept up the school agenda: some headteachers, now legally bound to report results, have begun to use them as an indicator of school performance and are devising ways of improving standards. There were clear examples of teachers modifying the content and style of their teaching; this did not appear to reduce in 1993 with the 'boycott' (in fact, many Y2 teachers did a considerable amount of assessments, but did not report them to the LEA), or with the government's withdrawal of its commitment to school league tables at ages 7 and 14. Nevertheless, the Midboro adviser revealed that in 1993 and 1994 there had been some loss of momentum with the changes and that there had:

> not been a dramatic increase in the quality of teaching because things like the boycott had stopped teachers from thinking it through.

Impact on assessment practice

By 1993, the 11 remaining Y2 teachers all felt they had improved their understanding of assessment. For three of them, it was just a feeling of being 'more relaxed and confident' or 'growing more adept at TA'; but for the other eight, improved understanding had meant changing their assessment practices. Some of these changes were linked to whole-school development (often led by our teachers) and some were personal changes the teachers were making. In some cases we can look at these changes in relation to the models of TA described in Chapter 2.

Changes in assessment practice

In 1993, eight of the 11 remaining Y2 teachers from our original sample of 32 said they had made changes to their personal ways of working. These changes involved the ways in which they were assessing children.

Two teachers said that they were paying much more attention to the role of questioning in assessment. The first was conscious of asking more questions of children. She also wanted to let the children in on the assessment process: to let them know they are being assessed (for example, in science AT1) on how investigative and enquiring they can be, which means telling them they have to ask questions like 'but what if we changed this or that? So she was consciously trying to get the children themselves to pose more questions about the experiments they were doing. While teaching history, the second teacher realized that she had to be 'more subtle' in her questioning. She reported learning that 'you restrict children by closed questions' and 'you can just say to them "tell me what you know" and get more out of them'. Generally, while assessing other areas, she had been focusing on asking more open-ended questions, 'trying to get more spontaneous comments from them' and trying 'to get them to say what they know'.

Two teachers said they were doing more observation. The teacher mentioned above who was getting children to pose more questions said she was concentrating more than ever on observing children, particularly in relation to maths:

> Definitely more change. There was a feeling that our general maths results were weak last year. I am trying to record more

rigorously. This means a change in assessment techniques – doing much more observation. I am recording every day now in maths.

Two other teachers were conscious of 'writing more down', part of the shift from intuitive to evidence-based assessment. One had begun to write more on each piece of children's work; an example of this would be:

> I am pleased to see you have now begun to use a capital on the word England.

She called these 'my cryptic comments' and they serve as a message to the child and the parents and as a memo to herself when she is scanning through the exercise books before writing reports. For another teacher, one of our evidence gatherers, 'there is more writing down of assessment than there used to be'. This had been the main change in her assessment practice: 'taking much more detailed notes than before'. She was not so clear about the audience for these notes, but their main purpose was to boost the evidence she has – she kept them alongside annotated pieces of work.

At a school which was very critical of national assessment, the teacher was now trying to 'build in' assessment, rather than 'leaving it' as she used to:

> For every AT covered, for each SoA, I'll think of a couple of assessment activities and give them to the children at the end of the time spent on that area.

This is indeed a change in attitude for this teacher, but it is personal. The staff have always worked in 'their own individual ways' and 'nobody would be forced to use anything ... we don't do things that way'.

For the last two of these eight teachers, focusing more closely on SoAs and getting used to specific criteria had been the main change.

Overall, rather than the importance of national assessment dropping off in 1993 with the boycott, the 11 teachers had been thinking more about assessment in 1993. The schools with systematic planners became more systematic in their planning for school development in assessment: all these schools made changes in both whole-school and personal assessment practices. In three of the systematic schools there was strong evidence of the raised professionalism of Y2 teachers through their leadership in assessment issues and INSET across the school. In schools with evidence gatherers and intuitives, there was less organized development and less focus on the 'nitty-gritty', such as criterion referencing using SoAs. The teachers (except for those in two schools) were not really using results to change their practice, but were at the stage of accepting national assessment and focusing on what it had meant for them personally:

> Looking back, it was better to give it a try and see what the problems were, rather than simply refusing to do it and not knowing.

Whole-school policy development

In 1993, responses from the 11 teachers who remained from our original sample of 32 indicated whole-school developments in three schools, and in each case the developments were led by Y2 teachers whom we had judged to be systematic planners. These developments involved the organized use of old SAT materials across the school, organized practising of assessment skills by all the teachers and whole-school changes to teachers' planning in order to encompass assessment.

Using previous SAT materials to do TA had become part of the practice of two schools. In one case, the SAT materials have been added to a bank which included teacher-developed assessment tasks. (When teachers hit upon an activity that is a particularly good way of assessing a SoA, they write it up and store it; other teachers can then use the task instead of inventing their own.) Junior teachers in the school have been given the last two years' SAT materials and our Y2 teacher produced some guidelines for them: for example, how to do a level 3 number assessment; how to 'apply criteria' (as in level 4 spelling).

At the other school (possibly our most systematic), the head-teacher had suggested that the SAT materials, accumulated over three years, be used to advantage, to plan for assessment across the school. He argued:

> After all, the SAT materials cover levels 1–4 which represents the whole age range of pupils at this school.

In addition, there had been more departmental meetings and more cross-phase meetings (infant/junior) which focused all teachers' attention on 'evidence of attainment' as outlined in the SAT guidance; the science co-ordinator ran INSET on assessment of ATI, using 'evidence of attainment' from previous SATs. This corroborates the work of Herman and Golan (1994), who found that one of the effects of standardized testing on teachers was that teachers often looked at prior test materials.

As a case study in practising observation, all the teachers at the first school mentioned above were setting a task in science and 'sitting back trying to observe ATI'. They were trying to decide and agree what might be considered as evidence of attainment in some of the SoAs which are harder to assess, for example, when a child is 'making related observations'.

At the first school, as an outcome of working with our Y2 teacher, the junior teachers were planning assessment into their forecasts and saying how they would go about it. Similarly, to ensure a whole-school approach and to help non-Y2 teachers to 'home in on assessment', all teachers at the second school mentioned above had been given new planning sheets developed by the assessment leader (our Y2 teacher). The headings were as follows:

AT
Level
Activity
Resources
Type of group/whole class
Kind of assessment
Which SoA

This is a detailed level of planning and points to giving time to assessment during the school day, thus suggesting that the entire staff became systematic planners, if not daily assessors. It also illustrates how teachers make sure that their plans cover objectives that will be tested (Herman and Shari 1994). At a third school, our Y2 teachers were asked to work with junior colleagues in the planning and assessment of science 'because our experience of taking Y2 for three years will be needed'.

By 1994, at the time of writing, we had interview data from 19 of the headteachers from our original study and from our contacts in the four LEAs. Four of our headteachers had been against SATs from the beginning and championed TA or the PLR. In these schools there had been little or no reported policy development. In another nine schools, headteachers had got policies in place; these schools have the following in common:

- They all think national curriculum assessment has been a good thing.
- They have built it into their plans in different ways (some doing assessment tasks at the end of a topic, some using old SATs at specific times).
- The teachers all work to the system.
- Teachers and heads report improved TA ('far more rigorous due to the criteria being applied'; 'we did it in our heads now we are used to assessing against levels').
- Teachers consult and use passed-up records ('for making groups'; 'to take children on'), according to the heads.

In all nine schools there was consistently one person in addition to the head who had been through the procedures for the past four years (either the Y2 teacher or someone who had helped with SATs).

A further three schools had a lot in common with those mentioned above, but there was one main difference – the teachers were not required to work to the same system; this may have something to do with heads' beliefs either in the teachers' judgement:

> The teachers still continue to do assessment the way they have always done – as a class teacher, you know instinctively when a child is ready for the next stage.

or in preserving individualism:

> Teachers don't work in a similar way. There are no diktats in this school about the regularity or type of assessment.

Three of our original headteachers were still not happy about the state of assessment practice in their schools. One (whose Y2 teacher had left) felt that there was 'a much clearer understanding' but:

> we are nowhere near where we should be – we would be more effective if we were better at it.

Another, whose Y2 teacher (a tried and tested methodologist) had retired and whose Y6 was a new deputy, was brutally honest:

> I can't honestly say our methods of assessment have improved because we are still trying to get to grips with it. We find it very

difficult and don't have enough knowledge to put a child at a level.

Across her school assessment was:

> Very hit and miss, very hit and miss. Not good, no sorts of similarities, no coherence, nothing.

The head of the newly amalgamated school (who had originally been in our sample of Y2 teachers) thought that, despite having imposed a pro forma on the staff to ensure planned-in assessment, they would simply conjure up their memory at the end of a term:

> When it's time to fill in the records, they think, 'Right, he can do that, he can do that'.

Neither would they take a child on from where the last teacher placed him or her:

> not many people bother to look at passed-up records: some take hearsay, some look at exercise books, some purely look at reading age, some don't look at anything – they wait and see.

The advisers gave us a picture of assessment across their local authorities. Overall, although awareness had been raised and there was more understanding about assessment, practice in schools varied considerably. In Innercity it varied enormously from school to school:

> Some schools have got very enhanced forms of record-keeping and sampling systems in place and some of our schools will even be noting on an AT and level as evidence. In other schools, that won't be the case and the schools will quite openly say to you, 'We'll need to get systems in place and we are without a policy'. So we are talking about a very wide continuum.

Similarly, Northshire reported:

> We know that there are some schools where there has been a certain amount of heads in the sand for a very long period of time, and on the other hand we've got some institutions where they have continued to work very hard – they've monitored the performance of children since they came into Key Stage 2, they've used the assessment information from Key Stage 1, and they are looking to prepare children to move into Key Stage 3.

In Midboro:

> There was a different level of discussion from previous
> years. There was much more understanding of what criterion
> referencing meant and there are people using the kind of
> assessment language they wouldn't have done a few years ago.

The adviser thought that LEA INSET, together with the creation of
assessment co-ordinators in schools, had a lot to do with OFSTED's
recent report that assessment at Key Stage 1 had improved. Likewise
in Homeshire:

> Criterion referencing is now fairly embedded. This has
> evolved through schools being involved in agreement trialling.

In addition:

> Y2 teachers are much superior in terms of speed at levelling a
> piece of work and are quicker at recognizing national curri-
> culum criteria within children's work.

Impact on teachers

It became obvious that most of our respondents had seen the
introduction and implementation of national assessment as some
kind of ordeal because they wanted to talk about the effect it had
had on teachers themselves. Some described it more dramatically
than others (and they all used weather metaphors): 'it's a cloud on
the horizon' and 'we've ridden the storm'. The most graphic des-
cription came from the head of a first school in Homeshire:

> An avalanche hit us! We may have needed the snow but not
> that much and not at that speed. If it hadn't been for my strong
> teachers we would have gone under.

After three years of national assessment, one clearly positive outcome was perceived: the collegiality referred to in Chapter 4 was
still evident as increased co-operation between teachers. Five heads
declared that doing assessment had led to 'more co-operation'
between teachers and themselves:

> It has made us get together and discuss how you would look
> for progress.

Heads are a lot more open when you go along to meetings.
Before, everyone pretended that everything was hunky dory,
whereas now they are much straighter. We are all in the same
boat so we've all got to help each other.

There has clearly been an impact on assessment practice in
most of our 19 NAPS 1 schools since 1990. At the time of writing
(1994), there is a reported all-round 'heightened awareness' of
assessment.

The contribution of Year 2 teachers

One of the themes which emerged from the data was the raised professionalism of Y2 teachers. Their consciousness had been raised
and their assessment practice enhanced by their involvement in the
very first years of national curriculum assessment. While many of
our original Y2 teachers had left or moved on, in 1994 five of our
primary heads who continued with the second study, NAPS 2,
stressed the contribution that these Y2 teachers were making to
assessment at Key Stage 2. One head had simply moved his Y2
teacher into the Y6 slot (and indeed four of our 32 Y6 teachers had
been Y2 teachers in the recent past). Three others reported that Y2
teachers had shared their methods and helped to ease Key Stage 2
teachers into the idea of national curriculum assessment:

Key Stage 1 teachers and Key Stage 2 teachers have shared
methods.

Junior teachers are certainly benefiting from Y2 colleagues.
They don't feel as isolated.

The Year 2 teacher has been working with the Year 6 teacher
who has complete confidence in her, so there is no level of
anxiety there.

One of our infant school heads said that the Y2 teacher was helping
her with assessment throughout the school, and advisers in the four
LEAs generally agreed that heads were using the expertise of Y2
teachers.

Both Northshire and Innercity advisers made the point that if a
school was a primary and was used to whole-school planning then
Y6 teachers (and others) were likely to have benefited. Two Y6
teachers expressed their gratitude:

I think one of the best things was talking to our colleagues who were involved in Key Stage 1 SATs.

I've had tremendous support from the Key Stage 1 teacher. She has passed her expertise up the school.

There have been other developments at school level (either self-instigated or guided by the LEAs) which involve analysing national assessment results, more agreement trialling and moderating of children's work and the development of school portfolios and school policies.

Across the four LEAs, advisers reported that, although there is some '*ad hoc* work' and 'a sprinkling of agreement trialling going on between schools', there was much more going on in individual staffrooms. Teachers were getting together and looking at and moderating pieces of work. (This was corroborated by five of our Y6 primary teachers.) Besides this, all four LEAs have organized formal meetings which give teachers the opportunity to share views and assign levels. This does not mean, however, that all teachers have attended.

By the end of the NAPS 1 project, nearly all our schools were using some kind of SoA checklist as a summative yearly record for each child. Some of these were 'customized' as headteachers wanted to 'keep in the elements we valued' (although it must be said that most were based on a popular purchased record with every SoA listed.) A few used the PLER either by itself or in conjunction with a national curriculum checklist. Schools which had built in time for assessment or sampling had numerous other assessment sheets which were kept in children's folders as evidence.

Is national assessment bedding down?

In 1994, teachers from 19 schools and four LEA advisers, who had witnessed the progress of national curriculum assessment over the period of three and a half years, described the impact it had made upon them and their schools: it had brought teachers closer together but at the same time had taken its toll, mainly adding to their workload and to the pressures of everyday life. We heard from head-teachers that there had been changes in teaching methods and classroom organization and a tendency to narrow the curriculum and concentrate on the core and the tested subjects; other research which focused directly on the curriculum indicates that it is non-national curriculum subjects – art, PE, music and RE – that have suffered as a result (Campbell and Neill 1994; Pollard *et al.* 1994). At the same time there had been a varied amount of development in school assessment practices. The question remained as to whether national curriculum assessment had in fact been accepted and embedded into teachers' and schools' ways of working.

There was a general feeling from the eight Key Stage 1 schools still being studied in 1994 that things had grown easier over the previous four years. Teachers were 'more *au fait*', 'more familiar with the procedures', some were using old SATs for TA and despite the fact that LEA 'support had dwindled' in two LEAs, SATs had grown more manageable and easier to administer. Some Y2 teachers who were 'experienced SATters' were sharing their expertise with the rest of the staff and Y6 teachers felt that 'the infants have got it all in place' and 'they are spot on! They are not frightened, they've been used to it.' At least five schools had systems in place with which they were comfortable and they were analysing their results.

For ten of our 19 primary schools, SATs were 'still a disruption', expensive if extra help was bought in, and resented because they had become paper and pencil (whereas 'the very first SATs supported proper teaching' and were 'very informative about children's learning'). Over the years, ten of the 19 headteachers had taken the results of SATs quite seriously and had endeavoured to use the results to target areas of weakness from one year to the next. As part of a whole-school policy they had tried to ensure that teachers themselves used results to take children on.

Both heads and advisers told us how some teachers had retired or resigned possibly as a result of having to do national assessment. Clearly, others soldier on:

> The will is there. There is no doubt about that. They will work and they will get all the processes in place if they can.

And others have survived:

> We've ridden the storm. We've come to terms with it. We've accepted it. We made the best job of it.

> An avalanche hit us and we dug ourselves out.

8

CONCLUSIONS:
INTUITION
AND EVIDENCE?

Raising standards

The first issue to consider is whether the national assessment programme has raised 'standards' and, if so, how. Many educational
innovations are adopted, even though there are high levels of uncertainty about their outcome; this is particularly true in the case
of using testing programmes to raise standards. The legitimacy of
assessment programmes derives not from empirical evidence of
their likely effectiveness but from the perceptions that they evoke,
together with the symbolic order and control which they offer
(Airasian 1988). The standards issue is routinely couched in terms
of certification and exam passes, and traditional moral values.
Because of this symbolism, testing to raise standards strikes a
responsive chord with the public at large which helps to explain
the widespread and speedy adoption of this particular form of
innovation, Airasian argues. The traditional values which the
testing programmes endorse are the same as those endorsed by the
majority culture, and this is the legitimization necessary to justify
their widespread adoption. This argument about the moral element
of the introduction of testing programmes is particularly interesting

in relation to what has happened in England and Wales where a return to traditional teaching and traditional examinations is, in the view of the extreme right, linked with reasserting traditional moral values: the 'back to basics' theme. The re-emergence of the traditional examination is clearly on the agenda. With the added feature of central control, together with sanctions for poor performance, the symbolic importance of any testing programme will be increased. The argument is that regardless of the actual impact that such high-stakes tests have, they are seen to have an important impact by the public at large. Of course, the public's perception of the power of such tests to raise standards can be supported: in such a situation teachers will teach to the test and so students' scores will rise. In Britain, as we pointed out in Chapter 1, exactly this claim was made in 1991 with regard to the introduction of the national curriculum.

In only the second year of national assessment the government was indeed able to show that standards had risen: the then Secretary of State for Education, John Patten, held a press conference at the end of 1992 proclaiming raised standards, since the percentage of the seven-year-old population reaching higher levels had risen in reading, spelling and maths ('Seven-year-olds' results show improving standards', DfE press release, 21 December 1992). Patten took this as evidence that the national curriculum was 'working'. From our study we would say that this rise in levels of performance was due to teachers teaching more of what was required in the SATs: punctuation, spelling, handwriting and mental arithmetic. There was more attention to 'the basics' in 1992 and 1993, and this showed up in the children's improved levels of performance. The experience of doing the SATs also helped teachers to understand the SoAs so they could teach in a more focused way in later years. However, given the changes in the curriculum and to the assessment tasks in each of the three years, together with the lack of dependability of results (Shorrocks *et al.* 1992), we are inclined to say that such changes in patterns of performance should be treated with caution. Furthermore, as we show in Chapter 7, the processes which had brought about what headteachers saw as improvements in teaching, were complex and not just to do with the imposition of external tests. Interestingly, Campbell and Neill's (1994) research with 100 Key Stage 1 teachers who were members of the Association of Teachers and Lecturers reports that, in 1993, almost half these teachers felt that standards achieved by their pupils had improved in science, technology, history and geography; 20% felt standards had risen in English and maths (while 30% thought standards of reading had fallen). Only 20% felt standards had improved overall.

We can theorize at a more detailed level about how and why teachers changed their practice by looking at the literature on the effect of high-stakes testing programmes on teaching. 'High stakes' means that the results have a significant impact on either pupils' or teachers' lives: stakes can be high either for the students or the teachers, and in some cases both. Whether concerned about their own self-esteem or their students' well-being and prospects, teachers aim for their pupils to perform well on high-stakes tests, thus teachers spend a significant amount of their teaching time on the school work assessed by such tests. A high-stakes test, therefore, serves as a powerful 'curricular magnet' (Popham 1987: 680).

In England and Wales the aim of the national curriculum and assessment programme was not particularly to change teaching, but to drive up standards. The general implication was that this would be done through more 'rigorous' and traditional teaching and this was made explicit in the report of the 'Three Wise Men' (Alexander *et al.* 1992). As Chapter 6 showed, our teachers were concentrating more on the basics of spelling, handwriting and mental arithmetic, thus in relation to one of the key questions at the beginning of this book, it is clear that standards of performance in the basic skills have risen, but not simply because of the introduction of testing; the league tables also had an effect. The opprobrium heaped on LEAs that were at the bottom of the LEA league table in 1991 and anxiety in schools about having poor results also meant that there was pressure to produce higher performance in 1992.

One major concern about test-driven teaching is that scores on tests may rise because teaching is aimed at particular test items or questions and it is not necessarily the case that the broader underlying skill or knowledge covered is improving (Linn 1981; Madaus 1988). In the USA the practice of teaching to the test in order to raise test scores is called 'test-score pollution'. The 'pollution' here refers to an increase in test score which is not connected with improved skill in the construct or skill being measured. This is what Linn (1981) refers to as improving test scores without actually mastering the skills or constructs being assessed. The important question is whether the skills taught in practice for the test are narrowly or broadly conceived. What our NAPS teachers were doing was not generally teaching directly to specific test items (although children were doing 'quick' mental arithmetic in order to be able to do sums in the test within five seconds), but teaching areas of the curriculum so that their children could do assessments on those topics. The difference between the situation which we have been observing and that in most other countries, where teaching to the test is observed, is that in England and Wales we have an imposed curriculum as well as imposed testing. There is, therefore, something other than tested items for teachers to teach towards. In addition, the assessment tasks have changed each year and there has been a rolling programme of attainment targets included in the testing, so teachers cannot easily become too narrow in preparing pupils for the tests. The few examples of taking home handwriting patterns for practice and making sure that certain topics were taught before the SAT activity seemed to be essentially ones of timing and curriculum coverage rather than a pointed and narrowing teaching to the test. It seems, therefore, that we were *not* witnessing narrow teaching to the test, or 'test-score pollution' in our Key Stage 1 schools, but a more broadly conceived modifying of curriculum and teaching, together with an improvement of assessment practice. However, we feel there is a grave danger that as the scope of the tests shrinks, such narrow teaching may happen in future.

In a study similar to this one in the USA, Mary Lee Smith (1991) worked over 15 months in two elementary schools looking at the effect of the introduction of testing on teachers' lives and practice. Smith's work on the effects of testing on elementary teachers has significant overlap with some of our findings. Some of her findings are as follows:

1 The publication of test scores produces feelings of shame, embarrassment, guilt and anger in teachers and the determination to do what is necessary to avoid such feelings in future.
2 Beliefs about the invalidity of the test, together with the requirement to raise scores, set up feelings of dissonance and alienation.
3 Beliefs about the emotional impact of testing on young children generate feelings of anxiety and guilt among teachers. (Smith

points out that not all teachers feel this way and administrators tend to deny emotional effects on pupils or blame pupils' emotional responses on the overreaction of teachers.)

4 Testing programmes reduced the time available for instruction.

Smith's first two points were echoed in our study and seem to be powerful factors in the reaction of teachers of young children to the requirement to carry out formal high-stakes testing. Our work in the early 1980s found widespread standardized testing in primary schools, but little hinged on the results of such testing (Gipps *et al.* 1983). Results were generally entered in teachers' record books, allowing the LEA to keep a benevolent eye on primary schools, and sometimes helped in the identification of children for remedial help. That is very different from the requirements of the national assessment programme as we observed it.

Feelings of anxiety and guilt were features of, particularly, the first year of national assessment in Y2 classes. It may be that some of the teachers overreacted, but they were genuinely concerned about the effect of formal testing and published results on their pupils.

A reduction in the time available for teaching was clearly also the case for the national assessment programme in England and Wales; the only advantage of the testing programme in this respect is that the activities in which the children were engaged for the assessment were, particularly in 1991 and 1992, activities which were not, on the whole, wasting their time, but interesting, classroom-related activities, which many of the children enjoyed (Pollard *et al.* 1994). There was, however, a diminution in the quality of experience for children not being tested.

To sum up, our findings echo Smith's in a number of ways: the feelings of anger and guilt about the published results, and heads' and teachers' intention to avoid this in future; feelings of dissonance and alienation because of the perceived invalidity of the testing programme; and feelings of concern about the impact of testing on young children. What we also observed, however, in some schools was heads and teachers taking charge of the innovation and using it in line with their beliefs about good professional practice.

Intuition or evidence?

What was the balance of intuition to evidence in the early stages and how did this develop? Chapter 2 describes how schools and Y2 teachers began to develop policy and practice in relation to teacher assessment. Much of this early focus was on developing record sheets and systems of recording rather than on the process of assessment itself. We found initially that teachers were generally unable to explain to us how they made their judgements about whether children were at a particular level or could 'do' an SoA. This was important to us as a research question and because of our intuition or evidence theme: to what extent were these teachers' judgements analytical and evidence-based and to what extent intuitive? Since the Dearing Review in 1994, teachers are being encouraged to make very global judgements, in terms of whether children's performance is closer to one set of level descriptions than another, and again they may make these on the basis of evidence carefully considered, or intuitively.

One practice that emerged was the collection of evidence to support teachers' judgements; some teachers, our evidence gatherers, kept everything while others kept a carefully selected range of work. Another practice was ticking boxes: many schools bought a record-keeping system which consisted of every SoA listed with boxes beside them for teachers to tick when a particular child had attained a particular SoA. Observation, to ascertain whether children could do certain things or were using particular skills, also emerged as a developing practice; observation of this kind, together with questioning of children, is a key element of formative assessment. Such observation can be systematically planned and carried out against a list of criteria (as with our systematic assessors) or carried out in a more global way. It is our view that the experience of doing the early SATs helped teachers to develop these observation and questioning skills: in the SAT assessment situation teachers had to give children tasks to do which were planned to assess specific criteria, they observed children's performance against these criteria and were given examples of questions to ask to probe understanding. For many of our teachers the activity of sitting with three or four children and observing and questioning them undisturbed for extended periods was a revelation, and while they could not maintain the time given to such closely focused observation, they were none the less conscious of the observation and questioning approach and tried to incorporate it into their practice. Clearly, the SAT alone was not responsible for this development in teachers' practice; in-service training from the LEA and guidance from the subject associations (for example, the Association for Science Education booklet ASE 1990) also contributed to this trend. Nevertheless, the SAT, which was envisaged by the TGAT report as moderating teachers' assessments, actually helped to develop teachers' skills in (formative) assessment – although it must be said that the TGAT report was emphatic that the SATs should embody good practice in teaching and assessment (Black 1993).

What our study shows clearly is the shift in Y2 teachers' assessment practice (notwithstanding individual variation) from an intuitive approach to one based on evidence and written records. Also, it is clear that the bulk of our teachers did become more knowledgeable in assessment rather than being technicians operating an imposed system. This came about, however, not because of having to give an external standardized test (as with Y6 teachers and the Key Stage 2 testing in 1994), but because of the demands of TA and the performance-type activities in the SATs. It was these requirements which, together with the (albeit too detailed) specification of the curriculum, had, in headteachers' views, led to an improvement in planning, teaching and assessing in Y2 classes. So we suggest that it was the broad scope and range of the national assessment programme at Key Stage 1 in the first three years that led to developments in teachers' practice. We do not intend to downplay the problems in the assessment programme, for there were many (overload, too many and yet inadequate assessment criteria, low levels of training, particularly for TA, lack of dependability of the results, etc.), but to make the point that if we wish to raise real standards of teaching and formative assessment (which in turn supports teaching and learning) then we need more than imposed external traditional tests (see also Torrance 1995).

One theme which we first came across in 1991 was the raised professionalism of Y2 teachers; this was reported in a third of our schools and involved Y2 teachers leading assessment training and policy development. By 1994 five of the 11 primary headteachers who were left from the original study (having continued through to the second stage of our research looking at Key Stage 2) stressed the contribution their Y2 teachers were making to assessment at Key Stage 2. The four LEA advisers all generally agreed that heads were indeed using the expertise of Y2 teachers.

Increased levels of discussion and collegiality were observed in our schools in the early stages of the implementation to support Y2 teachers who, it was felt, were faced with an awesome task; and among Y2 and other teachers throughout the study to negotiate meanings for SoAs and standardize judgements. Headteachers' involvement as moderators for the LEA or leading and supporting their staff meant that there was a feeling of 'being in it together' which also helped to develop collegial ways of working. Helping each other with SATs and moderating SATs and TA brought teachers out of their classrooms and into working contact with each other. By late 1993 heads (and Y6 teachers) were still talking of increased co-operation among teachers, and between teachers and heads, and of Y2 teachers sharing their expertise with other staff in the school. In primary schools it is fairly unusual for infant teachers to be leading developments at the top of the juniors, but this is indeed what has happened. This persistence of collegiality 'across time and space' indicates that it is indeed *not* contrived collegiality that we were observing, but the development of a more genuinely collaborative culture (Hargreaves 1994), albeit one born out of adversity.

Teachers and criterion-referenced assessment

If we take assessment against specific criteria as the key definition of criterion-referenced assessment, then in order for teachers to be carrying out criterion-referenced national assessment, they needed to be making assessments of children against assessment criteria, i.e. the SoAs. It also means that the evaluation of the pupils' performance (i.e. the grade awarded or in this case the level) has to be directly related to the achievement of the criteria, with no consideration given to the amount of effort put in, or to the extent of progress made. What we found with our teachers – and this was echoed by an NFER study (Lee 1993) – was that in the first two years only one-fifth were assessing routinely and formatively against the SoAs. Some teachers and schools had broken down the SoAs even further to make 'Can do' lists and were assessing and recording against these; for those teachers this seemed more effective than using SoAs. The question is why did teachers not use the SoAs? Was it just a question of the time needed to get used to them? Were there too many? (In which case, how did having 'can do' lists help?) Would they have done it if they had felt more committed to national assessment? Does a teacher have to be a systematic type of person in order to approach assessment in this way? Was it clear to teachers that they were supposed to be making assessment against the SoAs?

The answer is, probably, a bit of all these: teachers were not particularly committed to the national assessment programme, which they saw as an attempt to hold them accountable; they were certainly not given guidance and training in relation to how a criterion-referenced assessment might work, particularly in relation to the use of SoAs; the newness of the SoAs and their number meant that it would take time (two years?) for teachers to get to know them and to be able to use them 'intuitively'. It is interesting to consider why the 'can do' lists apparently did work: perhaps because the statements made more sense to the teachers (and were, therefore, more useful) and because the teachers had some ownership of them. This might suggest that the problem lay with the SoAs themselves, that they were not clear enough to be used for assessment purposes but needed to be broken down even further; such a line of thought leads us straight to the 'traditional' criterion-referenced assessment dilemma of too much specificity leading to overload and fragmentation of the curriculum. The SoAs were too numerous and yet not specific enough. This leads us on to a more fundamental question: is criterion-referenced assessment of this sort feasible and appropriate for teachers' classroom use within formative assessment?

Developments in criterion-referenced assessment elsewhere have tended to move away from over-specification towards a more holistic approach (Gipps, 1994); even Popham, one of the strongest supporters of criterion-referenced assessment in the USA, now argues in favour of stating only a few broad objectives (Popham 1987; 1993). In England and Wales attempts to develop grade-related criteria for the GCSE were abandoned in favour of more general grade descriptions. In the national assessment programme, too, the task of the Dearing Review was to ease the load for teachers, to simplify the curriculum structure and thus the assessment task; the result is that, in line with the general trend in criterion-referenced assessment, assessment will be against very general descriptions for each level rather than the SoAs. One advantage of having broad descriptions is that they can encompass more complex skills and processes than can detailed assessment criteria, so that assessing higher-order skills and processes is possible; a disadvantage of this very broadness is that it makes dependable, consistent assessment less likely, an important point if the assessment is to be used for accountability or evaluative purposes. The provision of exemplars – examples of work reaching particular levels – together with the provision of group moderation for teachers can help to enhance consistency in such a situation.

It remains to be seen whether the level descriptions will be useful in teachers' ongoing formative assessment. Indeed, what will teachers use as a basis for making their classroom assessment: the slimmed down curriculum itself in the Programmes of Study? Will they find that they have to make the equivalent of 'can do' lists again? Or will they make global, intuitive judgements, like our intuitive group?

But to return to our teachers and their experience of criterion-referenced assessment in 1991 and 1992, many of them found it difficult to evaluate the children's attainment and award a level *without* giving any recognition to factors such as behaviour, effort and progress. Some teachers were adamant that with young children such assessment was inappropriate and interfered with the teachers' attempts to maintain motivation and self-esteem. This again highlights an issue in relation to formative/summative assessment: teachers see positive feedback as an important aspect of formative assessment/teaching; if strict criterion referencing reduces the teachers' ability to provide such feedback, then it is likely that they will find it problematic, although it may be argued that the feedback to the child does not necessarily have to reflect the grade in the record book. In aggregating results to provide a final grade for public examinations, compensation – setting a good performance in one area against a poor performance in another – is usually allowed, thus reducing the strictness of the criterion referencing. This, however, is not the same issue that our teachers were facing: whether and how to allow 'compensation' for progress and effort. Another aspect with which our teachers struggled was that the intuitives and, to a lesser extent, the evidence gatherers, saw assessment against a list of SoAs, or 'can do' statements as 'too clinical'.

The point emerging seems to be that aspects of this model of criterion-referenced assessment were not acceptable to some of our infant teachers, particularly those who were intuitive and child-centred in their approach and philosophy. Research in the USA reports a similar finding (Brookhart 1993) that teachers incorporate effort into final grades because of their concern about children's self-esteem, and also because they find it hard not to do so for weak pupils who try hard. Teachers, in that study, saw grades as something that students earn and they would not separate out the uses of assessment from the grade awarded. For some uses, particularly the development of self-esteem, achievement and effort are both relevant constructs. On the other hand, the experience of some systematic assessors was that using the criteria had helped them to focus on the child's attainment and not to be distracted or affected by their problems or behaviour; for the systematic planners the teachers' knowledge of the child was used in teaching and assessing, but not in the actual final level awarded.

Assessing and learning with young children

We now look at the TA models and at how assessment practice is linked with views of teaching and learning. We should emphasize, however, that these are only models and relate to Y2 teachers in 1991 and 1992, i.e. at a particular stage in the national assessment programme; we are currently investigating the models over time and with Y6 teachers. We felt, based on our research evidence, that these assessment approaches which we grouped into models were related to the teachers' views of teaching and learning, their general style of organization and teaching, and their reaction to the imposition of national curriculum assessment. Teachers were thus developing assessment practice in line with their general practice and philosophy of primary education.

The intuitives rely on their memory in making and recording assessment so that there is a lack of observable TA. They do not refer to statements of attainment, they do not take notes, they reject systematic recorded assessment as too formal and structured an approach. For them only the teacher can assess the child; assessment is built on close, all-round knowledge of children. This group of teachers broke down into two subgroups. The first, the children's needs ideologists, have an exploratory or 'scaffolded' view of learning, in which they provide a stimulating environment and guide children towards discovering or learning. The second subgroup, the tried and tested practitioners, have a more didactic model of teaching and learning and they see assessment as assessing what is taught. Both subgroups resist assessment in relation to statements of attainment: the children's needs ideologists because it is in tension with a 'whole-child' philosophy, the tried and tested practitioners because it would mean a radical change in behaviour for them. These teachers continued to incorporate effort or children's performance in relation to their background factors when making an assessment; their resistance to criterion-referenced approaches is epitomized by their reluctance to internalize or to have readily available the statements of attainment. The tried and tested practitioners were essentially making summative assessments: they would sit down at the end of a term or half term and 'call up their memory' and record an assessment for each child in relation to each attainment target. The children's needs ideologists would say that they were constantly making formative assessments, (and may well have been) but they could not articulate this, neither was it visible. In carrying out their assessments, both of these subgroups made use of assessment procedures with which they were familiar, such as the ILEA Checkpoints, their own or school-developed worksheets and tests, and maths worksheets from published schemes. This was in spite of the fact that these results did not relate to the levels and attainment targets of the national curriculum.

The evidence gatherers collect evidence, written or drawn, in order to have a basis for making assessments. Some of these teachers collected enormous amounts of evidence. At the end of each term or half term, they would sit down and go through all the evidence and assign levels: evidence gatherers do not rely on memory, since they feel that they need more than that to make an accurate assessment. However, often there is too much evidence to be used, and the teachers do not interrogate it all; part of the reason for collecting so much evidence seems to be that the evidence proves that the national curriculum has been covered and is available to support the judgement of the teacher when and if it is called into question. In addition, collecting evidence in this way does not interfere with their normal teaching and classroom practice. These teachers tend to plan their work using the broad attainment targets and wait for assessment opportunities to arise rather than planning for assessment. The model of learning held by these teachers seems essentially to be a traditional, didactic model: children learn what is taught and only what is taught; assessment follows teaching to check that the process is going according to plan. These teachers' view of criterion-referenced assessment is interesting in that they understand the idea of assessment in relation to criteria, but insist that context and pupil's background must sometimes be taken into account in judging performance; again they do not use individual statements of attainment. For this group of teachers also, TA is essentially summative; however, this group is becoming aware of a range of assessment procedures and recognized the importance of observation, and of children's talk, in making informal assessments.

Both the evidence gatherers and the intuitives, rather than using SoAs, tended to have an overall notion of 'levelness' and, therefore, seemed to rely on implicit norms in judging children's performance. Some of the teachers, because of the quasi norm-referenced use of levels, tended to use level 3 to indicate children of well above average attainment. Thus they ridiculed the possibility that children might, at this age, be reaching level 4. Our observations, however, indicated that in some of the schools (and not always those in affluent areas) pupils were indeed able to achieve level 4 in some parts of the curriculum.

Systematic planners plan specifically for TA: they identify activities and tasks within their planned programme of teaching with specific SoAs in mind. They use multiple techniques for assessment: observation, open-ended questioning, teacher–pupil discussion, running records, scrutiny of written work. Of the two subgroups, systematic assessors and systematic integrators, the systematic assessors give daily, concentrated time to assessment and separate themselves off from the rest of the class to do it. For the systematic integrators, assessment is integrated with regular classroom work and often the teacher circulates around the class gathering her evidence in different ways. These teachers espouse and/or operate on a constructivist approach to learning: children learn in idiosyncratic ways and not always what is taught. They also have a particular view about assessment, which means that they are keen to arrive at shared meanings in relation to grading children's work with colleagues. They do understand and operate a model of assessment against criteria. They use SoAs openly and regularly, often broken down into more detailed 'can do' lists. Information about effort, progress and performance in relation to background goes into RoAs or children's personal records. The significant difference between this group and the other two lies in the use of SoAs by the former. These teachers seem to be carrying out formative assessment in that assessment feeds into their planning on a regular and systematic basis, the children's records are accessible and used (something which we did not see with the other two groups) and they see real value in continuous, formative assessment as enhancing their professional development and effectiveness as teachers. Teachers in this group do not necessarily maintain a model of formative assessment which involves making goals clear to the child, feeding back information directly related to those goals to the child, discussing and setting standards with the child and attempting to make them self-monitoring learners. In fact, this sort of feedback, in relation to specific national curriculum goals, or assessment criteria, was almost never observed in the Key Stage 1 classes where we worked.

We believe that these models are helpful in allowing us to see where primary teachers may be in their views about assessment in relation to the use of criteria and exemplars, since we see these as key issues for ensuring consistency and, therefore, quality in TA, particularly where it is to be used for reporting and accountability purposes.

Appropriate assessment

This approach to young children's learning and assessment was to a certain extent echoed by the Y3 teachers who received children and assessment information from our Y2 teachers. A small proportion (one-sixth in 1991 and in 1992) insisted that the Y2 teachers' *comments* gave them more useful information than the national assessment results; while the assessment results were useful, these teachers wanted more than the 'objective' results, they wanted subjective information from the previous teacher about individual children's character:

> in teaching terms you need to look at the whole child, PSE, etc.
> as part of the assessment.

So what these teachers wanted was more than assessment data; they wanted the sort of personal information that might be found in an

184 Intuition or evidence?

RoA. This, of course, is possible, but on top of national assessment it implies a large set of material being produced by the teacher and passed up.

Progression is another interesting theme. The national curriculum ten-level scale is designed to permit, indeed encourage, progression, with children working through the levels and being taken on by their receiving teachers without too much repetition. In the past there has been evidence that records and test results, though passed up, are little used (Clift *et al.* 1981; Gipps *et al.* 1983) either within primary schools or in primary–secondary transfer. Our work with Y3 teachers suggested that by the second year they were becoming more familiar with the levels and finding the assessment information more useful. On the other hand, some teachers who found the results useful nevertheless made it clear that they wanted to make a fresh start each year: they did not want their knowledge of the results to cloud their judgement of the children coming up to them. Some felt it was 'not right to look at the documents' before they knew the children, as this might prejudice their ideas towards the child at the beginning of term.

Schools' practice in letting children progress to level 4 was mixed; from 1992 seven-year-olds who were capable of attaining level 4 were to be allowed to work at this level and be assessed on it. Teachers' and advisers' views were varied and schools interpreted the LEA advice in a cavalier fashion, but overall 18 out of 32 schools did not offer any children the opportunity to take the level 4 tasks, suggesting that such a level of differentiation (level 4 is the level expected for most 11-year-olds) was difficult to envisage, or manage, for many teachers.

These things taken together – some teachers' reluctance to assess against lists of criteria; their belief that they wanted more than objective information about children; their reluctance to leave effort and progress out of the final grade/level; the belief that the SoAs were too clinical; the tendency to go for a 'fresh start' rather than building on the passed up results; and reluctance to use level 4 – illustrate these teachers' philosophy about appropriate assessment, teaching and learning for young children; furthermore, they demonstrate that the TGAT model for national assessment did not fit this philosophy. The TGAT model, which offered a criterion-referenced assessment with information passed up and built on to reduce overlap and aid progression (with RoA in the background as a device for recording personal information), was not what these primary teachers wanted. Even if it had been properly developed and resourced and not tied to competitive arrangements for accountability, we suspect that many teachers might still have objected to the systematic, 'clinical', 'objective' approach and the lack of focus on the whole child, because of their intuitive child-focused (rather than subject-focused) approach. However, we should note that the 'fresh start' philosophy is a widespread phenomenon, and the reluctance to see seven-year-olds performing at the level of 11-year-olds may be due to the practical difficulties in organizing for differentiated teaching in the classroom, rather than ingrained low expectations of pupil performance.

Either way, the TGAT model, though strong on concern about the impact of the national assessment programme on the primary curriculum, was not designed around existing primary teachers' practice and did not address the issue of how primary teachers with a strong intuitive, child-focused approach would react.

Conclusions

Our research indicates that there are specific issues related to the age of the children being assessed which mean that they require a particular type of assessment programme. For example, our teachers commonly tried to get the best performance out of the children by reassuring them, helping them, offering preparation and emotional support and sometimes even a second chance. Developments in educational assessment suggest that one aspect of a good assessment is that it elicits best performance (Wood 1986; Nuttall 1987; Gipps 1994) and that this adds to the test's validity. Our evidence from the NAPS study was that teachers tried in the assessment programme to elicit best performance from the pupils on the SATs, through encouragement, offering good conditions, etc. This, we felt, was not due to teachers' particular models of assessment but rather to their view of what is appropriate for children of this age. Teachers were concerned about 'failure' and 'labelling' for such young children and there was some tension between offering children the chance to try the next advanced level in the assessment programme, or indeed to keep plugging away at a particular assessment task, and the need to prevent the children experiencing failure. Our teachers also went to enormous lengths to hide the fact that testing was taking place; despite the stress and anxiety reported, there was very little of this observed when the children were being assessed (see also Pollard *et al.* 1994). The children were generally unaware of the purpose and importance of the tasks in which they were engaged. This was because the teachers were at great pains to ensure that they were protected from what was going on. Very few children were seen to be upset by the activities, some were bored but it was much more common that children enjoyed them. Furthermore, because many of these pupils performed better on the SAT than in the TA, this made the teachers think hard about their evaluation of the pupils.

It may also be the case that when teachers of young children assess those children, either individually or in small groups, it is almost inevitable that they will vary the way in which they introduce the task, whether they are given highly specific instructions or not; this is because what the teacher sees is not a testing situation but individual children whom she or he knows well and who need to have things explained to them in different ways, or presented in different ways, because of the children's own backgrounds, abilities and immediate past history. If this is the case, then it will not be possible (and, one might say, not desirable) to have standardized performance assessments with young children. This is a crucial issue if the level of difficulty then varies across children and tests are to be used for accountability purposes.

A number of other studies of national curriculum assessment at both seven and 14 (SEAC 1991b; Gipps 1992) indicate that the SAT, with its emphasis on active, multi-mode assessment and detailed interaction between teacher and pupil, may, despite the heavy reliance on language, be a better opportunity for many children, particularly minority and SEN children, to demonstrate what they know and can do than traditional, formal tests with limited instructions; in other words, that they elicited best performance (Nuttall 1987; Gipps 1994). The key aspects seem to be:

• a range of activities, offering considerable opportunities to perform;
• match to classroom practice;
• extended interaction between pupil and teacher to explain the task;

- a normal classroom setting, which is therefore not unduly threatening;
- a range of response modes other than written.

What, then, is likely to be the effect of the move towards more narrowly conceived standard tests? Of course, there is the concern over the impact of the paper and pencil format on teaching practice – narrowing rather than broadening it. Having said that teachers were glad the tasks were briefer, six of our heads were fearful that the paper and pencil format, 'which the government wanted', was regrettably creeping in while realizing that it was the schools' complaints about time that led to the new shorter format.

We'd be devastated if it goes back to paper and pencil.

The move from 'tasks' to pencil and paper 'tests' will force teachers back to formal subject-based teaching . . . will move pedagogy back to the 1950s.

We must also anticipate that a move to more formal standardized procedures will not elicit best performance in the same way, nor will the tests be as good an opportunity for many children, and in particular those whose first language is not English, or those with special needs, to show what they know, understand and can do (Gipps and Murphy 1994).

To conclude, we believe we have offered evidence that, as a result of the national curriculum and assessment programme, teachers have redirected the focus of their teaching and this has been reflected in improved national assessment results in the 'basic skills'. Greater care in planning, close observation of children and a more detailed understanding of individual progress impacting on teaching were reported by over half our headteachers, as well as a lasting effect on collaboration and discussion by a smaller number. Many of our Key Stage 1 teachers have moved away from intuitive approaches to assessment towards more systematic, evidence-based techniques. The SATs have acted as a training device, and group moderation has broken down barriers. There is a clear picture of enhanced understanding and practice in assessment for the Y2 teachers, and heads and LEAs are putting these skills to good use further up the system. All this has been achieved, however, at a cost to teachers' lives and ways of working. Finally, we believe our evidence shows that the improvements in practice, both in teaching and assessing, would not have resulted from the introduction of traditional standardized tests alone, but depended on a wider approach with moderated teacher assessment at its core.

The introduction at Key Stage 1 of the national assessment programme to raise standards has in many ways had the impact desired of it by government; but our evidence shows, we believe, the complex nature of this 'impact'. And that has very considerable implications for the impact of the national assessment programme for 11-year-olds at the end of Key Stage 2 based on standardized tests: without the same emphasis on moderated teacher assessment, and without the enhanced assessment skills and quality of information resulting from carrying out performance-based assessment tasks, the effects on teaching will not be so broad or, we would add, so valuable.

APPENDIX

NATIONAL ASSESSMENT IN PRIMARY SCHOOLS 1 PUBLICATIONS

Brown, M. L. (1991) Problematic issues in national assessment, *Cambridge Journal of Education*, 21(2).

Brown, M. L. (1993) Assessment in mathematics education: developments in philosophy and practice in the UK. In M. Niss, *Cases of Assessment in Maths Education*. Dordrecht: Kluwer.

Gipps, C. (1989) Quality in internal assessment. In W. Harlen (ed.), *Assuring Quality in Assessment*. London: Paul Chapman.

Gipps, C. (1995) Reliability, validity and manageability in large-scale performance assessment. In H. Torrance (ed.), *Evaluating Authentic Assessment*. Buckingham: Open University Press.

Gipps, C., McCallum, B., McAlister, S. and Brown, M. L. (1992) National assessment at seven: some emerging themes. In C. Gipps (ed.), *Developing Assessment for the National Curriculum*, Bedford Way Series, University of London Institute of Education. London: Kogan Page.

Gipps, C. and Stobart, G. (1993) *Assessment: A Teacher's Guide to the Issues* (2nd edn). London: Hodder & Stoughton.

McCallum, B. (1991) SATs and rites of passage, *British Journal of Curriculum and Assessment*, 2(1).

McCallum, B., McAlister, S., Gipps, C. and Brown, M. L. (1991) Something to gain? Creative responses to national assessment, *Aspects of Education*, 45: 18–25.

McCallum, B., McAlister, S., Brown, M. L. and Gipps, C. (1993) Teacher assessment at Key Stage One, *Research Papers in Education*, 8(3): 305–27.

McCallum, B., McAlister, S., Brown, M. and Gipps, C. (1995) National Curriculum assessment: emerging models of teacher assessment in the classroom. In H. Torrance (ed.), *Evaluating Authentic Assessment*. Buckingham: Open University Press.

REFERENCES

Abbot, D., Broadfood, P., Croll, P., Osborn, M. and Pollard, A. (1994) Some sink, some float: national curriculum assessment and accountability, *British Educational Research Journal*, 20(2).

ASE (1990) *Teacher Assessment. Making it work for the Primary School*. Hatfield: Association for Science Education / Association of Teachers of Mathematics / Mathematical Association / National Association for the Teaching of English.

Airasian, P. (1988) Measurement-driven instruction: a closer look, *Educational Measurement: Issues and Practice*, 7(4): 6–11.

Alexander, R., Rose, J. and Woodhead, C. (1992) *Curriculum Organisation and Classroom practice in Primary Schools: A Discussion Paper*. London: DES.

Audit Commission (1989) *Losing an Empire, Finding a Role: The LEA of the Future*, Occasional Papers No. 10. London: HMSO.

Ball, S. (1990) *Politics and Policy Making in Education*. London: Routledge.

Ball, S. and Bowe, R. (1992) Subject departments and the 'implementation' of the national curriculum, *Journal of Curriculum Studies*, 24(2): 97–115.

Bennett, S. N., Wragg, E. C., Carre, C. G. and Carter, D. S. G. (1992) A longitudinal study of primary teachers' perceived competence in, and concerns about, National Curriculum implementation, *Research Papers in Education*, 7(1).

Berman, P. and McLaughlin, M. (1977) *Federal Programs Supporting Education Change.* Santa Monica, CA: Rand.

Black, H. and Dockrell, W. B. (1984) *Criterion-Referenced Assessment in the Classroom.* Edinburgh: Scottish Council for Research in Education.

Broadfoot, P., Abott, D., Croll, P., Osborn, M., Pollard, A. and Towler, L. (1991) Implementing national assessment: issues for primary teachers, *Cambridge Journal of Education,* 21(2).

Brookhart, S. (1993) Teachers' grading practices, *Journal of Educational Measurement,* 30(2).

Brown, M. (1991) Problematic issues in national assessment, *Cambridge Journal of Education,* 21(2).

Brown, S. (1980) *What Do They Know?* Edinburgh: HMSO.

Campbell, J. and Neill, S. (1994) Curriculum Report at Key Stage 1: Teacher Commitment & Policy Failure. Harlow: ATL/Longman.

Clift, P., Weiner, G. and Wilson, E. (1981) *Record Keeping in Primary Schools.* London: Macmillan Educational Books/Schools Council.

Close, G. and Brown, M. (1987) *Graduate Assessment in Mathematics: Report of the SSCC Study Part 1: Summary and Evaluation.* London, DES.

Consortium for Assessment and Testing in Schools (1990) *The Development of SATs at KS1: A Report to SEAC.* London: SEAC.

Davidson, C., Leach, M. and Strachan, J. (1993) The school down the road: experiences with school-based and external assessment in New Zealand. Paper presented to IAEA Conference, Mauritius.

Dearing, Sir Ron (1993) *The National Curriculum and its Assessment. Interim Report, July 1993.* London: NCC and SEAC.

Denvir, B., Brown, M., and Eve, P. (1987) *Attainment Targets and Assessment in the Primary Phase: Report of the Mathematics Feasibility Study.* London: DES.

DES (1977) *Education in Schools: A Consultative Document.* London: HMSO.

DES (1985) *Better Schools,* Cmnd. 9469. London: HMSO.

DES (1987) *The National Curriculum 5–16: A Consultation Document.* London: HMSO.

DES (1988) *National Curriculum Task Group on Assessment and Testing: A Report.* London: HMSO.

DES (1991) *How is Your Child Doing at School? A parents' guide to testing.* DES leaflet.

DES (1992) How is your child doing at school? A parents' guide to tests and reports for 7 year olds. DES leaflet.

Fullan, M. (1982) *The Meaning of Educational Change.* New York: Teachers College Press, Columbia.

Fullan, M. (1991) *The New Meaning of Educational Change.* London: Cassell.

Gipps, C. V. (1988a) The TGAT report: trick or treat?, *Forum*, 31(1): 4–7.

Gipps, C. V. (1988b) What exams would mean for primary education. In D. Lawton and C. Chitty (eds), *The National Curriculum*, Bedford Way Papers no. 33. London: University of London Institute of Education.

Gipps, C. V. (1992) Equal opportunities and the SATs for seven year olds, *The Curriculum Journal*, 3(2).

Gipps, C. V. (1994) Developments in educational assessment or what makes a good test?, *Assessment in Education*, 1(3).

Gipps, C. V. and Goldstein, H. (1983) *Monitoring Children: An Evaluation of the Assessment of Performance Unit*. London: Heinemann Educational Books.

Gipps, C. and Murphy, P. (1994) *A Fair Test? Assessment, Achievement and Equity*. Buckingham: Open University Press.

Gipps, C. and Stobart, G. (1993) *Assessment: A Teachers' Guide to the Issues* (2nd edn). London: Hodder & Stoughton.

Gipps, C. V., Steadman, S., Goldstein, H. and Stierer, B. (1983) *Testing Children: Standardised Testing in Schools and LEAs*. London: Heinemann Educational.

Goldstein, H. and Cuttance, P. (1988) National assessment and school comparisons, *Journal of Education Policy*, 3(2).

Hargreaves, A. (1994) *Changing Teachers, Changing Times*. London: Cassell.

Hargreaves, A. and Woods, P. (1984) *Classrooms and Staffrooms: The Sociology of Teachers and Teaching*. Milton Keynes: Open University Press.

Harlen, W. (1983) *Guides to Assessment in Education: Science*. London: Macmillan.

Harlen, W. (ed.) (1994) *Enhancing Quality in Assessment*, BERA Policy Task Group on Assessment. London: Paul Chapman.

Havelock, R. (1969) *Planning for Innovations*. Ann Arbor Insitute for Social Research, University of Michigan.

Herman, J. and Golan, S. (n.d.) The effects of standardized testing on teaching and learning – another look. CSE Technical Report 334, UCLA.

HMI (1979) *Aspects of Secondary Education in England*. London: HMSO.

HMI (1991) *Assessment, Recording and Reporting*. London: HMSO.

Hord, S. (1987) *Evaluating Education Innovation*. Beckenham: Croom Helm.

Huberman, A. M. and Miles, M. B. (1984) *Innovation Up Close*. New York: Plenum.

Hughes, M., Wikeley, F. and Nash, T. (1994) *Parents and their Children's Schools*. Oxford: Blackwell.

James, M. and Conner, C. (1993) Are reliability and validity achievable in national curriculum assessment? Some observations on moderation at Key Stage One in 1992, *The Curriculum Journal*, 4(1).

Laroque, L. and Coleman, P. (1989) Quality control: school accountability and district ethos. In M. Holmes, K. Leithwood and D. Musell (eds), *Educational Policy for Effective Schools*. Toronto: OISE Press, pp. 168–91.

Lawton, D. (1992) Whatever happened to the TGAT Report? In C. Gipps (ed.), *Developing Assessment for National Curriculum*, Bedford Way Series/University of London Institute of Education. London: Kogan Page.

Lee, B. (1993) *Supporting Assessment in School: The Role of the LEAs*. Slough: NFER.

Linn, R. L. (1981) Curricular validity: convincing the courts that it was taught without precluding the possibility of measuring it. Paper presented at the Ford Foundation Conference, October, Boston College, MA.

Madaus, G. (1988) The influence of testing on the curriculum. In R. Tanner (ed.), *Critical Issues in Curriculum*, 87th Yearbook of NSSE Part 1. Chicago: University of Chicago Press.

Maslow, A. (1954) *Motivation and Personality*. New York: Harper.

Moustakas, C. (1967) *Creativity and Conformity*. New York: Van Nostrand.

Murphy, R. (1990) National assessment proposals: analysing the debate. In M. Flude and M. Hammer (eds), *The Education Reform Act 1988*. London: Falmer Press.

NFER/BGC Consortium (1991) 'A Report on the Pilot Study of SATs for Key Stage 1', unpublished report to SEAC.

NFER/BGC Consortium (1992) 'An Evaluation of the 1992 National Curriculum Assessment at KS1', unpublished report to SEAC.

Nuttall, D. (1987) 'The validity of assessments', *European Journal of Psychology of Education* 11(2): 108–18.

OHMCI/OFSTED (1993) *Assessment, Recording and Reporting – Key Stages 1, 2 and 3 Fourth Year, 1992–93*. London: HMSO.

Parnes, S.J. (1970) Education and creativity. In P. E. Vernon (ed.), *Creativity*. Harmondsworth: Penguin.

Pollard, A., Broadfoot, P., Croll, P., Osborn, M. and Abbott, D. (1994) *Changing English Primary Schools? The Impact of the Education Reform Act at KS1*. London: Cassell.

Popham, J. (1984) Specifying the domain of content or behaviours. In R. A. Berk (ed.), *A Guide to Criterion-Referenced Test Construction*. Baltimore, MD: John Hopkins University Press.

Popham, J. (1987) Two-plus decades of educational objectives, *International Journal of Educational Research*, 11(1).

Popham, J. (1993) The instructional consequences of criterion referenced clarity. Paper presented at AERA Conference, April, Atlanta, GA.

Prais, S. and Wagner, K. (1983) *Schooling Standards in Britain and Germany: Some Summary Comparisons Bearing on Economic Efficiency*, Discussion Paper No. 60 (Industry Series No. 14). London: National Institute for Economic and Social Research.

Sarason, S. (1972) *The Creation of Settings and the Future Societies*. San Francisco: Jossey Bass.

SEAC (1991a) *School Assessment Folder*. London: SEAC.

SEAC (1991b) *National Curriculum Assessment at Key Stage 3: A Review of the 1991 Pilots with Implications for 1992*. London: SEAC.

SEAC (1992) *National Curriculum Assessments Arrangements. Responsibilities for LEAs*, Circular 12/92. London: HMSO.

Shorrocks, D., Daniels, S., Frobisher, L., Nelson, N., Waterson, A. and Bell, J. (1992) *ENCA 1 Project Report*. London: SEAC.

Smith, M. L. (1991) Put to the test: the effects of external testing on teachers, *Educational Researcher*, 20(5): 8–11.

Smith, W. F. and Andrews, R. L. (1989) *Instructional Leadership: How Principals Make a Difference*. Alexandria, VA: Association for Supervision and Curriculum Development.

Thomas, N. (1990) *Primary Education from Plowden to the 1990s*. Basingstoke: Falmer Press.

Times Educational Supplement (1993) 'Dunce City' leads league table battle, TES, 28 February: 8.

Torrance, H. (ed.) (1995) *Evaluating Authentic Assessment*. Buckingham: Open University Press.

Wallach, M. and Kogan, N. (1970) A new look at the creativity–intelligence distinction. In P. E. Vernon, (ed.) *Creativity*. Harmondsworth: Penguin.

Whetton, C., Ruddock, G. and Hopkins, S. (1991) *A Report on The Pilot Study of Standard Assessment Tasks for Key Stage 1*, the NFER/BGC Consortium. London: SEAC.

Wood, R. (1986) The agenda for educational measurement. In D. L. Nuttall (ed.), *Assessing Educational Achievement*. London: Falmer.

INDEX

A FAIR TEST?
ASSESSMENT, ACHIEVEMENT AND EQUITY
Caroline Gipps and Patricia Murphy

How far is assessment fair? In this evaluation of research from a wide range of countries the authors examine the evidence for differences in performance among gender and ethnic groups on various forms of assessment. They explore the reasons put forward for these observed differences and clarify the issues involved. The authors' concern is that assessment practice and interpretation of results are *just* for all groups.

This is a complex field in which access to schooling, the curriculum offered, pupil motivation and esteem, teacher stereotype and expectation all interact with the mode of assessment. This analytical and comprehensive overview is essential reading in a field crucial to educators.

320pp   0 335 15673 8 (paperback)   0 335 15674 6 (hardback)

EDUCATION REFORM
A CRITICAL AND POST-STRUCTURAL APPROACH
Stephen J. Ball

This book builds upon Stephen J. Ball's previous work in the field of education policy analysis. It subjects the ongoing reforms in UK education to a rigorous critical interrogation. It takes as its main concerns the introduction of market forces, managerialism and the national curriculum into the organization of schools and the work of teachers. The author argues that these reforms are combining to fundamentally reconstruct the work of teaching, to generate and ramify multiple inequalities and to destroy civic virtue in education. The effects of the market and management are not technical and neutral but are essentially political and moral. The reforms taking place in the UK are both a form of cultural and social engineering and an attempt to recreate a fantasy education based upon myths of national identity, consensus and glory. The analysis is founded within policy sociology and employs both ethnographic and post-structuralist methods.

Contents *Preface – Glossary – Post-structuralism, ethnography and the critical analysis of education reform – What is policy? Texts, trajectories and toolboxes – Education, Majorism and the curriculum of the dead – Education policy, power relations and teachers' work – Cost, culture and control: self-management and entrepreneurial schooling – New headship' and school leadership: new relationships and new tensions – Education markets, choice and social class: the market as a class strategy in the UK and USA – Competitive schooling: values, ethics and cultural engineering – References – Index.*

176pp   0 335 19272 6 (Paperback)   0 335 19273 4 (Hardback)